# The
# BONO EAST REGION
## in Ghana

# The
# BONO EAST REGION
# in Ghana

## The Untold Story

CHARLES K. ADDO

# THE BONO EAST REGION IN GHANA
## THE UNTOLD STORY

*iUniverse books may be ordered through booksellers or by contacting:*

*iUniverse*
*1663 Liberty Drive*
*Bloomington, IN 47403*
*www.iuniverse.com*
*1-800-Authors (1-800-288-4677)*

*Because of the dynamic nature of the Internet, any web addresses or links contained in this book may have changed since publication and may no longer be valid. The views expressed in this work are solely those of the author and do not necessarily reflect the views of the publisher, and the publisher hereby disclaims any responsibility for them.*

*Any people depicted in stock imagery provided by Getty Images are models, and such images are being used for illustrative purposes only.*
*Certain stock imagery © Getty Images.*

*ISBN: 978-1-5320-6725-9 (sc)*
*ISBN: 978-1-5320-6726-6 (e)*

*Print information available on the last page.*

*iUniverse rev. date: 02/07/2019*

# Foreword

Following overwhelming outpour of calls from chiefs, politicians, and opinion leaders across certain parts of Ghana for additional political administrative regions to be created, President Nana Akufo-Addo did set up the Brobbey Commission of Inquiry.

Among the terms of reference for the Commission, per the 1992 Constitution, was to ascertain the veracity or otherwise of the existence of a "substantial demand" for the creation of new regions. The Commission recommended the creation of six new administrative regions in Ghana. On December 27, 2018, the Electoral Commission conducted referenda, per constitutional provision that resulted in overwhelming 'YES' votes.

Among the new regions was Bono East.

Narratives of major historical events of Ghana have often been handed down to latter generations in the form of the so-called 'oral tradition.' This leaves much room for distortion of facts with passage of time.

This book tells about the untold story behind the Bono East Region and the impressive contributions made by certain individuals. This will serve as their legacy so that future generations can read about those contributions and accord them their rightful place in history.

Charles K. Addo, PhD

# Acknowledgments

Writing a story book of a magnitude, such as the creation of a new region, is somehow akin to filing for bankruptcy. In both situations, one is confronted with what appear to be limitless debts. It is impossible for me to acknowledge individually the countless men and women whose ideas, financial support, morale support, and other contributions made this historic event of a Bono East Region a reality.

The criticisms that I received, while not always adopted, nevertheless were generally on the mark, and have added clarity and inclusiveness to the finished product. I am grateful to Mr. Edward Anane, CEO, *The Techiman Times* newspaper; and Mr. Eric Konadu-Yiadom, CEO, Eric Spy Construction Ghana Limited, Techiman.

I am also grateful to the following media organizations and union within the enclave of the Bono East Region: Classic FM, Asta FM, Akina FM, Winners FM, Free FM, *The Citizen Times* in Techiman; Akyiaa FM and Jerryson FM in Nkoranza; Adars FM and Duapa FM in Kintampo; Star FM in Atebubu; Alive FM in Yeji, and the GPRTU.

I also express my sincere gratitude to all Chiefs and traditional rulers, Municipal and District Chief Executives, and Members of Parliament in the Bono East enclave; Mr. Emmanuel Kwasi Anyimadu, Clerk of Parliament of Ghana; Mr. John Owusu Agyeman, Legal Consultant, Aduofua Chambers, Techiman; Mr. Prince Yaw Donyina, former Municipal Chief Executive, Techiman; Mr. Obed Asante, CEO, Ghana

Nuts Limited Techiman; Dr. Kofi Amoako-Gyampah, CEO, Amoako Healthcare City, Techiman; Dr. Kofi Opoku-Agyeman, CEO, Opoku Agyeman Hospital, Techiman; Mr. Joseph Adom, CEO, J. Adom Construction Limited, Sunyani; Mr. Danso Abeam, CEO, Ghana Link Network Services Limited, Accra, who made tremendous commitments to the cause of the Bono East Region project.

Charles K. Addo, PhD

# Contents

# List of Tables

# List of Figures

# CHAPTER ONE

## 1.1 INTRODUCTION

### 1.2 Why Create a Region?

In 1902, Ghana, then called Gold Coast had three regions or Colonial Territories namely, the Coastal Regions, Asante Region, and the Northern Territories. In 1956, Trans-Volta Togoland became part of Gold Coast through a plebiscite.

At independence in 1957, the regions became five, comprising of Ashanti Region, Eastern Region, Northern Region, Trans-Volta Togoland, and Western Region with their respective capitals at Kumasi, Koforidua, Tamale, Ho, and Cape Coast.[1]

Upper West Region became the youngest region to be created in 1983, when it was split out of the then Upper Region without any benefit of broad consultation through a referendum of the people residing within the region. This happened under the Provisional National Defence Council (PNDC) military government decree.

---

[1] "The Colonial era: British rule of the Gold Coast." (1994). Retrieved September 2, 2018, from, http://reference.allrefer.com/country-guide-study/ghana/ghana17.html

Growth in the number of political administrative regions has never been static in Ghana. It has constantly been changing depending upon a whole range of forces, including political, economics, and ethnic reasons.

Table 1 depicts the dynamic nature of region creation in Ghana.

**Table 1:** *Regions Creation in Ghana from Colonial to Post-Colonial Times (1902 – 2018)*

| Year | Regime Type | Number of Regions | Reason for Region | Region Names |
|------|------------|-------------------|-------------------|--------------|
| 1902 | Colonial | 3 | British hegemony and consolidation of rule. | Ashanti Protectorate, Gold Coast Crown Colony, Northern Territories |
| 1953 | Colonial | 4 | British rule: division of Gold Coast Crown Colony into Eastern and Western Provinces for administrative purposes. | Ashanti Protectorate, Northern Territories, Eastern Province, Western Province |
| 1956 | Colonial | 5 | Successful conclusion of a plebiscite incorporating Trans-Volta Togoland as Volta Region into Ghana. | Ashanti, Eastern, Volta, Northern, Western Regions |
| 1959 | British Crown (1957-1960) | 6 | Brong-Ahafo Region carved out of Ashanti and Northern Regions | Ashanti, Brong-Ahafo, Eastern, Volta, Northern, Western |
| 1960 | First Republic (1960-1966) | 8 | Upper Region carved out of Northern Region. Western Region split into 2: Central and Western Regions. | Ashanti, Brong-Ahafo, Central, Eastern, Volta, Northern, Western, Upper Regions |

| 1982 | Military Rule (1982-1992) | 9 | Establishment of Greater Accra Region from Eastern Region | Ashanti, Brong-Ahafo, Central, Eastern, Volta, Northern, Western, Upper, Greater Accra Regions |
|---|---|---|---|---|
| 1983 | Military Rule (1982-1992) | 10 | Upper Region split into 2: Upper East and Upper West Regions | Ashanti, Brong-Ahafo, Central, Eastern, Volta, Northern, Western, Upper East, Upper West, Greater Accra Regions |
| 2018 | Fourth Republic (2017-2020) | 16 | Brong-Ahafo Region split into 3: Bono East Region and Ahafo Region. Western Region split into 2: Western North Region and Western Region. Volta Region split into 2: Oti Region and Volta Region. Northern Region split into 3: Savannah Region, Northern East Region, and Northern Region. | Ashanti, Central, Eastern, Northern, Western, Upper West, Upper East, Greater Accra, Bono East, Brong West, Ahafo, Savannah, Northern East, Western North, Oti, Volta Regions |

Source: Report of the Commission of Inquiry into the Creation of New Regions (June, 2018, p. 15)

There was much uproar by sections of Ghanaians regarding the wisdom in the creation of six new regions in Ghana under the Akufo-Addo government. Some had voiced their concerns that it was informed by political expediency, intended to rig the presidential elections in 2020.

Some too were are of the opinion that resources should rather be channeled towards Municipal, Metropolitan, and District Assemblies (MMDAs) because they constituted the real drivers of decentralization and socio-economic development.

Others even petitioned the Supreme Court for constitutional interpretation of the process for creation of a region because they thought the process was flawed and unconstitutional.[2]

Yet others argued that the creation was well past due since Ghana's population has grown significantly.

Among the general rationale that drives the creation of new regions are (a) economic viability, (b) ethnic and community interests, (c) meeting administrative convenience, and (d) reducing distance between the regional capitals and remote areas.

Of these, probably geographic distance holds the most prominent position, as it not only helps with better implementation and monitoring of government programs within the districts, but also better maintenance of order by law enforcement agencies in remote areas.

For, without effective maintenance of law and order, citizens can hardly go about their normal economic activities that ultimately results in socio-economic development.

## 1.3 Industrialization as Driver of Region Creation

The reasons why political administrative regions get created has been a major challenge for social science. They involve complexities in economics, political, and endless array of forces.[3] In less industrialized countries, and for that matter Ghana, the reason may partake of a broad process

---

[2] "New regions: Supreme Court throws out constitutionality suit". (2018). Retrieved November 30, 2018 from, https://www.ghanaweb.com/GhanaHomePage/NewsArchive/New-regions-Supreme-Court-throws-out-constitutionality-suit-704371

[3] Storper, M. (2010), "Why do regions develop and change? The challenge for geography and economics." *Journal of Economic Geography*, Volume 11, Issue 2, pp. 333–346. Retrieved September 1, 2018 from, https://academic.oup.com/joeg/article/11/2/333/1162217

of industrialization as a result of spatial dynamics of population and economic activity.[4]

Probably, the impetus that resulted in the creation of the new regions may very well be an encounter between two dynamic passions: strong petitioners' demand for a new region and a government that was completely committed to rapid industrialization of Ghana.

It was, as a result of a government that was in a calculated "hurry"[5] to industrialize the country, and impatient for the slow grinding forces of spatial dynamics, such as population and economic activity to dictate the pace of the region creation.

Also, spatial extent of the regions, especially from their regional capitals, may have been a major factor in the creation. It was unprecedentedly done within constitutional provisions of the 1992 Constitution.

This quest for industrialization by the government is made quite obvious when seen from the standpoint of its ambitious industrialization policies, such as the one factory in every district and the unprecedented commitment towards revamping the railway sector by extending it to the farthest part of the North of Ghana.

As one observer noted, region creations in Ghana are largely driven by the usual and frequent demands that are grounded in (a) political, (b) historical, and (c) ethnic factors.[6]

---

[4]  Black, D. & Henderson, V. (1999). "A theory of urban growth." *Journal of Political Economy*, 107, pp. 252–284

[5]  Ibrahim, A. (2017) "I am a man in a great hurry - Akufo-Addo" Retrieved September 2, 2018 from, http://www.myjoyonline.com/politics/2017/february-21st/I-am-a-man-in-a-great-hurry-akufo-addo.php

[6]  Be-Awuribe, S. (2017). "The Creation of Additional Regions in Ghana and Matters Arising." Retrieved August 30, 2018 from, http://ghananewsonline.com.gh/creation-additional-regions-ghana-matters-arising/

Of those reasons, the political reason often emerges as the most frequently cited, such as 'speeding up socio-economic development by bringing governance closer to the doorsteps of the local people.'

However, somehow couched in diplomatic language are detailed reasons often placed under the catch all phrase of "political reason."

These include among others, (a) unequal developments within the existing regions; (b) desire for political and cultural hegemony; (c) development policy failures; (d) practical geographic and administrative challenges; (e) desire for ethnic representation in national government; (f) real or perceived dominance of one or the other ethnic group in regional affairs; and (g) historical suspicions.[7]

There is no denying the fact that Municipal, Metropolitan, and District Assemblies (MMDAs) are the real drivers of local socio-economic development. One reason is that they do have dedicated sources of funding to cater for developmental programs. For instance, MMDAs do have the District Assembly Common Fund (DACF).

This dedicated fund, which varies from year to year, was 5 percent of the projected total national revenue for year 2017. It is based upon a formula that is periodically reviewed and approved by Parliament under the 1992 Constitution.

Among the factors that are considered in this formula are whether the District has education service, water availability, health service, tarred road, and the level of internally generated funds.[8]

Allocating national resource for socio-economic development is also informed by defined administrative institutions, such as sector ministries, departments, schools, hospitals, and other state institutions within a region.

---

[7] Ibid.

[8] "Parliament Approves 2017 Formula for Distribution of DACF." Retrieved September 10, 2018 from, http://www.commonfund.gov.gh/index.php?option=com_content&view=article&id=334&Itemid=440

Therefore, by creating regions, a whole new set of such state administrative institutions would be replicated within the new region, which attracts dedicated national funding that help boost the local economy to improve living standards.

Furthermore, creating and devolving power to new regions do affect population dynamics, as industries and businesses establish branches or expand their operations to those regions. This swells up the population of existing districts within those regions.

The resultant effect is that those that become too big get split up into two or even more depending upon the population density. Thus, the newly created District Assemblies join the existing ones to spread socio-economic development across the country through local governance. This helps fulfill the core mandate of districts, as drivers of decentralization.

Some of those reasons do enjoy the support of the 1992 Constitution. For example, equitable ethnic representation across all the regions, such as cabinet appointments and security service appointments, are much easily achieved if there are more regions.

Since no conclusive empirical evidence has yet been adduced for or against the creation of a new political administrative region, perhaps it may be the best course of action to leave the interplay of politics, economics, and endless range of forces to forge what posterity could only be the judge.

## 1.4 The Background Wrangling

It is fair to recognize those through whose efforts the Bono East Region was created, and to accord them their rightful place in history. This will ensure that future generations are not deprived of the contributions of the real actors.

The idea of creating regions in Ghana to accelerate the pace of socio-economic development was well entrenched in the 2016 Manifesto of the New Patriotic Party (NPP). It was an idea that floated around among some party members within the affected areas, quite possibly even before it found its way into the party's manifesto.

As far back as June 2016, before the December 7, 2016 Presidential and Parliamentary elections, the then Director of Elections of the major opposition political party, the NPP, Mr. Martin Adjei-Mensah Korsah, had discussions with the then NPP Presidential Candidate, Nana Akufo-Addo, on the possible creation of a new region for the eastern corridor of the Brong Ahafo Region, as part of those to be created in the likely event of an NPP victory.

Nana Akufo-Addo, was firmly convinced that he could bring about these new regions, even though no government has been able to do so using the relevant constitutional provisions. He believed that creation of new regions would help accelerate the socio-economic development process in the intended areas, and an NPP government ought to lead this charge and take credit for it.

He also believed that Ghanaians within those enclaves would be eternally grateful if such new regions were created, and could even result in voter sympathy and loyalty that could translate into more votes during elections for the NPP.

He was further cognizant of the fact that the creation of the last region of Upper West in 1983 had brought about a fair amount of socio-economic development to the people of that region.

It is fair to surmise that any rational individual, given the chance, would certainly want to be remembered years beyond one's transition from earth. What lasting public good did one leave behind as legacy? That is the essence of 'immortality.' It is an opportunity for one to be transformed into 'Andromeda' in the highest heavens.

Probably, Mr. Martin Adjei-Mensah Korsah might have grasped this essence and opportunity for 'immortality' through this region creation project.

However, the creation of the Bono East Region had not been among the many petitions and agitations that places like the Ahafo, Oti, Savannah, North East, and Western North had pushed for over several decades. Whereas that of the Bono East may have been fairly new, its case and need for a region was not in any way at variance with those of the other five regions, if not even dire.

On December 21, 2016, shortly before his appointment as Deputy Minister of Regional Reorganization and Development, Mr. Martin Adjei-Mensah Korsah conferred with the paramount chief of Techiman, Nana Akumfi Ameyaw IV, and other chiefs about the Bono East Region project.

The initial reaction to the idea was generally one of repulsion. From purely traditional perspectives, some of the chiefs believed a new region could divide and weaken the front of the Bono States. Probably, it was the early days and some chiefs and some politicians felt they had to tread cautiously until things became much clearer.

It was initially viewed from the position that such creation would be detrimental to the interests of the Bono States, because as it will wane in disunity and division, others like the Ashanti kingdom will remain intact and united. This would increase the hegemony of the Ashanti kingdom.

Other actors, acting independently of each other, but with the common objective of achieving a region in the eastern corridor, were also busy working underground. Among them were Nana Afena Nketia II (formerly called Mr. Fred Zeini), the Twafohene of the Techiman Traditional Area and Nana Apenten Fosu Gyeabour II, the Banmuhene of the Techiman Traditional Area. Later, other chiefs became persuaded and joined the bandwagon.

Now bearing an official tag as Deputy Minister for Regional Reorganization and Development, a ministry whose task it was to oversee the creation of the new regions, Honorable Martin Adjei-Mensah Korsah, could not have been in any better position to help bring about the much needed Bono East Region to help his people achieve rapid socio-economic development. At least, there was no constitutional provision against giving any support he felt would be needed.

The situation of Martin Adjei-Mensah Korsah may be essentially similar to the case in the 2000 US Presidential campaign when a TV journalist confronted George W. Bush with the question: "you've gotten to where you are in this presidential race because your father was president." His response was swift: "but I am also entitled to contest for the presidency in my own right as a citizen. The fact that I am his son doesn't take away my right to contest."

In the same vein, the position of Martin Adjei-Mensah Korsah did not preclude him from assisting his people to achieve rapid socio-economic development.

# CHAPTER TWO

## 2.1 THE INITIAL MOVES

### 2.2 The Bi-Partisan Nature of the Move

The clamor for a Bono East Region took the combined efforts of traditional authorities, political functionaries, and the people generally in the affected areas through a referendum. No sooner had it started than it quickly gained bi-partisan support and traction, turning into a collective objective.

The sense of a new region's potential to transform the socio-economic lives of the people was not lost on the people in the affected areas.

According to the Deputy Minister of Regional Reorganization and Development, Honorable Martin Adjei-Mensah Korsah, majority of Ghanaians supported the creation of the new regions.[9]

This observation by the deputy minister was buttressed by a former National Democratic Congress (NDC) Western Regional Minister, Honorable Paul Evans Aidoo, who observed that the sheer total land

---

[9] "'Most Ghanaians support creation of new regions' – Adjei Korsah".(2018). Retrieved August 29, 2018 from, https://www.ghanaweb.com/GhanaHomePage/NewsArchive/Most-Ghanaians-support-creation-of-new-regions-Adjei-Korsah-664160

area of some regions did not permit effective monitoring, evaluation, and many other activities by the Regional Coordinating Councils, which were constitutionally mandated to perform those functions.

Therefore, the problem of underdevelopment was not only one of limited resources, but also the absence of smallness and manageability of some of the regions.[10] Some regions were just logistic nightmare to scout, and Brong Ahafo was one of them.

One other analyst who also shared the above perspectives cautioned that cost should not be a major consideration. He argued that the creation of additional regions was need-based and not for political expediency. Citing the example of the ever expanding demand for schools, colleges, polytechnics, universities, health facilities, social amenities and many more due to a surge in population, he submitted that the existing centralization of projects at few centers or regions cannot meet those demands.[11]

Significant number of traditional authorities, political party opponents, and masses of people bought into the argument for a Bono East Region.

Call it the far shot dream that became a reality on December 27, 2018. On Tuesday June 20, 2017, two sub-chiefs Nana Apenten Fosu Gyeabour II, Banmuhene of the Techiman Traditional Area (and Hansuahene), and Nana Afena Nketia II (formerly Mr. Fred Zeini), Twafohene of the Techiman Traditional Area initiated a formal process that was to lead to the creation of the Bono East Region. It was carefully orchestrated with par excellence diplomatic skills. Destiny too may have played a role in the process.

Nana Apenten Fosu Gyeabour II, from business point of view, is the owner of Encom Hotel in Techiman.

---

[10] Ibid.

[11] Kipo, D. (2018). "There is need for creation of new regions in Ghana and cost must not be a limitation." Retrieved August 29, 2018 from, https://www.myjoyonline.com/opinion/2018/April-17th/there-is-need-for-creation-of-new-regions-in-ghana-and-cost-must-not-be-a-limitation.php

I had spoken with Nana Apenten Fosu Gyeabour II on several occasions. I remember I had visited him in April 2017 in connection with my bid to become the Brong Ahafo NPP Regional Chairman.

During that visit, Nana had advised that I solicit the support of the then Brong Ahafo Regional Minister, Honorable Kwaku Asomah-Cheremeh. My response was that I had already consulted him and also knew him personally.

I had consulted Honorable Asomah-Cheremeh during the exploratory stages of my campaign. This was because he had been the immediate past occupant of the very position that I was seeking to occupy.

He was the Brong Ahafo NPP Regional Chairman for nearly eight years when the party was in opposition. At my meeting with him, he was candid and forthright that the delegates would consider me as an "outsider," which I understood as someone who had never before held any party executive position. For that reason, they may be reluctant to give me their votes.

Interestingly, he himself was also an 'outsider.' But he probably won because the party was then in opposition and the competition may not have been all that keen. After all, whoever won during that time in opposition inherited the burden of financing the party from one's own resources out of opposition.

And so, I did find out when I abysmally lost the election on April 22, 2018 at the Pastoral Center in Sunyani. In fact, the trend of the voting nationally suggested a general delegates' inclination to retain the incumbent executives who had labored for the party with their own scanty resources while in opposition. The delegates probably felt it would be ungrateful to remove the incumbent executive en mass, now that the party was in power.

I got to know much about Mr. Asomah-Cheremeh when my book, *Returning the elephant into the city: the unfinished contract with Ghana*, was published in March 2015. I had liaised with him to help get it launched to raise funds for the NPP on July 18, 2015 by the then NPP Presidential Candidate Nana Akufo-Addo at the Tyco City Hotel in Sunyani.

This attempt to launch the book proved a major disaster as my Special Guest of Honor, Nana Akufo-Addo, and Chairman for the occasion, former President John Kufuor, travelled outside the country some few days to the event. The launching had to be postponed.

Figure 1 presents the announcement of the book launching postponement.

***Figure 1:*** Announcing the postponement of the first attempt of the book launch.

At the unsuccessful book launch: Dr. Charles Addo (right) and Honorable Kwaku Asomah-Cheremeh, the then Brong Ahafo NPP Regional Chairman and now Minister of Lands and Natural Resources (left) announcing to the few invited guests who turned up for the event that the event had been postponed indefinitely at the Tyco City Hotel, Sunyani, July 18, 2015.

For the Special Guest of Honor, Nana Akufo-Addo, I had been informed earlier by his then Political Assistant and now Deputy Chief of Staff, Mr. Francis Asenso-Boakye that he would be in Europe on the planned day of the launching.

Later, I learnt that Nana's agenda for that European trip was to lobby the European Union to support the NPP's call to have the bloated 2016 voters' register purged.

As to the Chairman for the book launching occasion, former President Kufuor, word had gotten to me from Honorable Charity Dwommoh, who is now the Tain District Chief Executive and then a colleague lecturer at the Catholic University College: The former President was travelling outside the country to the US some five days before the book launching event.

I had requested Charity to take up the assignment of introducing the Special Guest of Honor, now President Akufo-Addo, on the day of the book launch, so she was probably monitoring the movements of the invited VIPs to the event.

I had also requested Mrs. Vida Korang, a then colleague lecturer and a very good friend of mine, to introduce former President John Kufuor as the Chairman for the occasion.

To exacerbate matters, the date for the launching, July 18, 2015, had inadvertently coincided with the Muslim Eid al-Adha or Sala as it is commonly called in Ghana. This coincidence could not have been avoided because it depended on the day the moon actually is first sighted in the skies, as I understood the Muslim tradition.

This celestial observation had actually occurred, some two days earlier to the launching event. But for some unknown reason, the Sala was postponed to a date that coincided with the book launching.

The implication was that almost all of the then 124 minority Members of Parliament at the time that I had invited to the event also had very plausible reasons, as politicians, to excuse themselves: "There is a Zongo community everywhere in Ghana, and if I don't visit my constituency to celebrate with them, they may become resentful and penalize me at the impending elections."

That appeared to be a general excuse from almost all the invited Members of Parliament. Their Parliamentary Election was scheduled for December 7, 2016. Those excuses were relayed to me by Mr. Henry Baiden, Secretary of the Minority Members of Parliament, whom I was closely working with.

Some feelings of frustration began to creep into my world, especially after receiving several taunting anonymous text messages, such as "the elephant belonged to the bush!" and "where are your invited guests? Go find them in the bush."

It is quite likely that the writers of those messages got to know that my VIPs were going to be absent because the event was widely publicized in the *Daily Graphic* Newspaper of July 8, 2015, which included a contact phone number.

As expected, I incurred substantial financial losses; hotel venue rental, meals, and a whole range of expenses in connection with the preparations towards the event.

I had almost given up on this whole idea of launching the book when, some four months later, I read the news about the intention of Nana Akufo-Addo to officially outdoor his campaign team on December 19, 2015 at Sunyani. That presented me with yet another opportunity. I sought assistances from some members of The Tertiary Students Confederacy (TESCON), the students' wing of the NPP of Catholic University, of which I was the patron. They included Mr. Patrick Nketiah.

Subsequently, the book launching event was finally performed at the Sunyani Technical University Conference Center on December 18, 2015. Because it was also a fund-raising event, I donated the proceeds to the party, through Mr. Asomah-Cheremeh.

Figure 2 shows the successful book launch by the then NPP Presidential Candidate Nana Akufo-Addo.

***Figure 2:*** The successful book launch by the then NPP Presidential Candidate Nana Akufo-Addo.

At the successful second book launch attempt (From Left to Right): Honorable Afisa Djaba Otiko, then NPP National Women Organizer and former Minister for Gender and Development; Dr. Charles Addo, (Author), Ashanti Region NPP Chairman Bernard Antwi Boasiako (aka Chairman Wontumi), Nana Akufo-Addo, then NPP Presidential Candidate and now President of the Republic of Ghana; Mr. Stephen Ntim, NPP National Chairman Aspirant and former NPP National Vice-Chairman; Honorable Dr. Kofi Konadu Apraku, former MP and former Minister of Trade. Sunyani Technical Conference Hall, December 18, 2015.

Having made those contributions, including donating state-of-the-art meetings hall for constituency executives, donating free bus service to party members to maximize voter turnout on the election day of December 7, 2016, sponsoring or adopting polling stations, among others to the party, I somehow felt that I had 'paid my dues' and 'earned the rite of passage' to contest for the Brong Ahafo NPP Regional Chairman position. Besides, the position had been declared vacant, following the appointment of Lawyer Asomah-Cheremeh as the Regional Minister when the party won power.

Later, I learnt that in party politics, it is usually those who can lobby the hardest, not those who can sweat the hardest, that get to become recipients of recognition. A 'god-father' of some sort can be handy in order to advance in this game of 'hardball.'

And by 'hardball,' as Christopher Matthews, author of the renowned book, *Hardball*, defined it, "is clean, aggressive Machiavellian politics. It is the discipline of gaining and holding power, useful to any profession or undertaking, but practiced most openly and unashamedly in the world of public affairs."

Unfortunately, the reality is that in every political party, the members are just too many for everyone to get political appointment at the same time. Besides, life itself is a game of seasons, differing among individuals. One individual's winter may be another's summer. Certainly, people do not get to be born together, grow together, play together, work together, get same opportunities together, and die together. Natural law simply does not support or operate in that way of simultaneousness.

The other sub-chief that initiated the process for a Bono East Region was Nana Afena Nketia II (aka Mr. Fred Zeini). As mentioned earlier, he is the Twafohene of the Techiman Traditional Area. From business point, Nana Afena Nketia II operates a conglomerate of businesses, including ownership of Classic 91.9 FM radio station, bottled drinking water company called *Life Mineral Water*, and F. Zeini Trading and Construction, all within the Techiman Municipality. Nana knew something about the mechanics of campaigning because he had once sought for the position of a member of the Council of State representing Brong Ahafo Region.

The two explicit objectives that had taken Nana Apenten Fosu Gyeabour II and Nana Afena Nketia II to meet with the President of Ghana, Nana Akufo-Addo, at the Jubilee House in Accra were first to congratulate him for winning the 2016 Presidential elections. The second had something to do with an alleged ongoing legal tussle between the Techiman Traditional

Council and the Techiman Municipal Assembly. As in any human institutions in Ghana, the relationship between Traditional Councils and District Assemblies has not been one without conflicts every now and then.[12]

There was an implicit objective as well. The two chiefs may have seen their visit as offering a prime opportunity to discuss the issue of having a region in the eastern corridor of Brong Ahafo created. After all, region creation prominently featured in the 2016 Manifesto of the now ruling New Patriotic Party (NPP).

Bi-partisan promises by presidential candidates to create new political administrative regions in Ghana, in response to voters' requests in certain areas, are not uncommon during political campaign seasons.

They became hot issues in the run up to the December 2016 presidential elections that brought the NPP to power. Then ruling National Democratic Congress (NDC) government promised to create five additional regions if they got re-elected, while the then opposition NPP in turn promised to create four if they got elected[13].

The fact that both Parties went promising to create new regions did not come as much of a surprise. Usually, in their zeal to win votes from certain political enclaves, politicians do promise much, including probably the moon, if that could be possible.

The petitions already submitted for new regions included Oti Region, to be carved out of the Volta Region; Ahafo Region, to be carved out of the Brong Ahafo Region; and Western North to be carved out of the Western Region. The others were North East and Savanna Regions, to be carved out of the Northern Region.

---

[12] Asante, R. & Gyimah Boadi, E. (2004). "Ethnic Structure, Inequality and Governance of the Public Sector in Ghana." Retrieved September 5, 2018 from, http://www.unrisd.org/80256B3C005BCCF9/search/8509496C0F316AB1C1256ED900466964

[13] Dowokpor, W. (2018). "Creation of six new regions – Signs of a failing state?" Retrieved on August 26, 2018 from, https://www.myjoyonline.com/opinion/2018/June-29th/creation-of-six-new-regions-signs-of-a-failing-state.php

Up until this time, there had not been any formal petition for a Bono East Region, even though most analysts would probably agree that the Brong Ahafo Region was just too big, even without the Ahafo component.

As usual, upon their arrival in Accra, the two chiefs were joined by their two Members of Parliament from Techiman South and Techiman North who were resident in Accra, for the meeting with the President.

One was Honorable Martin Oti Gyarko representing Techiman North, and who also happened to be the biological son of Nana Apenten Fosu Gyeabour II. The other was Honorable Henry Yeboah Yiadom-Boachie representing Techiman South.

As members of the Legislature, both lawmakers naturally wielded some degree of influence, when it came to matters of having audience with the President of Ghana. They certainly brought those influence to bear on the visit to see the President.

On an official visit such as this one by chiefs, it was usual to have in their company a young man, Mr. Isaac Bonse Kwain, a nephew of Nana Afena Nketia. Mr. Kwain had appeared on the 2018 Brong Ahafo NPP Regional Party ballot as a contestant for the position of Regional Youth Organizer.

They were also joined at the Jubilee House by Madam Lawrencia Owusu, an NPP Women Organizer for the Techiman North Constituency, as well as Mr. Godson Afena Oti, a Director at Encom Hotel and also a biological son of Nana Apenten Fosu Gyeabour II.

Figure 3 shows the meeting with President Akufo-Addo by the entourage of Chiefs from Techiman.

***Figure 3:*** Group picture of the chiefs from Techiman with President Akufo-Addo after a Bono East Region petition meeting at the Jubilee House.

The President H. E. Nana Akufo-Addo (center) flanked by (from left to right) Madam Lawrencia Owusu (NPP Women Organizer for Techiman North Constituency); Honorable Yiadom-Boachie (MP Techiman South); Nana Afena Nketia II (aka Mr. Fred Zeini), Twafohene of Techiman Traditional Area; Mr. Godson Afena Oti (Director, Encom Hotel); Nana Apenten Fosu Gyeabour II (Banmuhene of Techiman Traditional Area and Hansuahene); Honorable Martin Oti Gyarko (MP Techiman North); and Mr. Isaac Bonse Kwain (2018 Brong Ahafo NPP Regional Youth Organizer Aspirant).

On Tuesday June 20, 2017, the entourage of the chiefs from Techiman arrived at the Jubilee House at around 6:00 PM. The president had been quite busy meeting with foreign ambassadors from different countries and his schedule had been very tight during the day.

He had just finished accepting the credentials of four envoys to Ghana and a host of other official engagements. By the time he got to meet with the chiefs' entourage it was night fall, around 9 PM. Of course, the president quickly apologized to them for keeping them waiting for so long. The chiefs went straight with their mission.

It was towards the end of their discussions with the President that the subject of petitioning for a Bono East Region cropped up. The president had received and compiled petitions, ready for onward transmission to the Council of State for advice, as prescribed by the 1992 Constitution.

That was when Nana Afena Nketia II (aka Mr. Fred Zeini) raised the issue about the large land area of the Brong Ahafo Region, even after the split off of the Ahafo enclave.

Nana Afena Nketia II suggested that if the president was really committed to his policy of bringing governance to the doorstep of the people, then carving out the Bono East Region from what remained of Brong Ahafo, after Ahafo was removed, may enhance the socio-economic development of the Bono East Region.

The President could not have agreed any better with Nana Afena Nketia's suggestion. Having recently come off the campaign trail to win the presidency in the far flung areas of the Brong Ahafo Region, the President probably understood better what Nana Nketia was driving at regarding the vast expanse of the Brong Ahafo Region.

His campaign trail had taken him through Brong Ahafo towns such as, Yeji, Kajeji, Kwame Danso, Atebubu in the Eastern part to Nkrankwanta, Wamfie, Dormaa Ahenkro, Berekum, Sunyani, Sampa, Drobo, Menji, and Banda towards the Western and Northern part of the region, to mention only a few.

This sheer land size of Brong Ahafo Region, in addition to Techiman, Nkoranza, Kintampo, and Wenchi, which lied towards the central part of the region must necessarily shrink resources for economic development and deprive other parts of the region of development. This must necessarily be so, given that resource allocation is done equally on regional basis.

"This is your time, Nana [i.e., Nana Afena Nketia II], if you want a new region for your people," the President said approvingly. He had only a week remaining, that is Tuesday June 27, 2017, to submit the petitions received so far to the Council of State for advice. His advice to the chiefs was, as a matter of urgency, submit a petition for him to include along those ready for submission to the Council of State.

Upon their return from Accra, after meeting with the President, Nana Apenten Fosu Gyeabour II and Nana Afena Nketia II briefed the Paramount Chief of Techiman about the new development. On Saturday June 24, 2017, the Deputy Minister for Regional Reorganization and Development, Honorable Martin Adjei-Mensah Korsah, called Nana Afena Nketia II to inform him that the president had called him in connection with their petition. His Excellency wanted to know whether the chiefs really meant business with their request, and if so, then they should expedite action.

It was still Saturday, June 24, 2017, while attending a major funeral ceremony when this news of the President's call reached Nana Afena Nketia II through the deputy minister. He recognized the urgency of the matter, and relayed the information at once to Nana Apenten Fosu Gyeabour II and Nana Twi Brempong II. The three sub-chiefs conferred with Nana Akumfi Ameyaw IV at the funeral grounds, and they decided to hold an emergency meeting at the palace of the Paramount Chief.

The outcome of that meeting was that the Registrar of the Techiman Traditional Council, Mr. Evans Eghan, was directed to compose a petition that night, as a matter of urgency, to be presented to the presidency in Accra.

## 2.3 The Tentative Petition

On Sunday, June 25, 2017, a tentative petition containing only five signatories that could be gathered in the heat of the moment was put together by the Registrar of the Techiman Traditional Council. It included the paramount chiefs and presidents of the following traditional areas.

Nana Pimampim Yaw Kagbrese V of Yeji and President of the Brong Ahafo Region House of Chiefs, Nana Akumfi Ameyaw IV of Techiman, Nana Owusu Akyeaw Brempong II of Atebubu, Nana Owusu Takyi II of Bassa, and Nana Obrempong Kru Takyi of Abease.

This petition was to hold place pending consultations for further and better petition containing more signatories.

This tentative petition was passed around by Nana Apenten Fosu Gyeabour, Nana Afena Nketia, Nana Twi Brempong, and the Registrar to those substantive paramount chiefs in the affected areas who could be reached.

Figure 4 shows the tentative petition.

**Figure 4:** The Tentative petition containing five signatories.

# COALITION OF CHIEFS FOR BONO EAST REGION

*P. O. Box 4*
*Techiman B/A*
*Ghana W/A*

*TEL: 0204343716*

*Our Ref. BONO EAST/PRES./VOL.1/01*

*Your Ref. No..........................*      *Date:*    *JUNE, 2017*

HE NANA ADDO DANKWA AKUFO-ADDO
THE PRESIDENT OF THE REPUBLIC OF GHANA
FLAF STAFF HOUSE
ACCRA.

## PETITION TO PARTITION BRONG AHAFO REGION
### RE: CREATION OF NEW REGIONS IN GHANA

We the undersigned Chiefs are Paramount Chiefs from various Traditional Areas in the Brong Ahafo Region in the Republic of Ghana and respectfully write to appeal to His Excellency; the President of the Republic of Ghana, Nana Addo Dankwa Akufo-Addo to partition and create three (3) new Regions in the Brong Ahafo region in order to bring Governance closer to the people considering the total geographical land Area of the Brong Ahafo Region.

Furthermore, Nananom appeal to His Excellency to use his good Offices to have the Brong Ahafo Region partitioned in order to enhance Infrastructural development, increase Economic opportunities as well as promote effective Governance in Ghana our Motherland.

We wish to point out the long distance between District Capitals in the Eastern Corridor of the Region and the present Capital, Sunyani

It is our hope that His Excellency will give serious consideration to our request.

Thank you.

PIMAMPIM YAW KAGBRESE V
PRESIDENT OF BRONG AHAFO REGIONAL
HOUSE OF CHIEFS AND OMANHENE OF
YEJI TRADITIONAL AREA

OSEADEEYO AKUMFI AMEYAW IV
OMANHENE OF TECHIMAN TRADITIONAL AREA

NANA OWUSU AKYEAW BREMPONG II
OMANHENE OF ATEBUBU TRADITIONAL AREA

NANA OWUSU SAKYI II
OMANHENE OF BASSA TRADITIONAL AREA

OBREMPONG KRU TAKYI II
(OMANHENE/PRESIDENT)
ABEASE TRADITIONAL COUNCIL

OBREMPONG KRU TAKYI II
OMANHENE OF ABEASE TRADITIONAL AREA

Meanwhile, a planning committee was formed to fine tune the "Coalition of chiefs for the Bono East Region." This saw Nana Bafour Asare Twi Brempong II, Adontenhene of Techiman Traditional Area, emerging as the Chairman of the Coalition; Professor Ameyaw Akumfi, as the Secretary; Nana Afena Nketia II, Twafohene of Techiman Traditional Area, as the Treasurer, and Nana Apenten Fosu Gyeabour II, Banmuhene of Techiman Traditional Area, as an Advisor.

On Monday June 26, 2017, the tentative petition reached the presidency through Mr. Evans Eghan, the Traditional Council Registrar, with the facilitation of the Deputy Minister for Regional Reorganization and Development, Honorable Martin Adjei-Mensah Korsah.

A final petition was subsequently presented to the Council of State, through the presidency, containing much broader signatories of chiefs and detailed justifications for a Bono East Region. It was passed around for signatories by Mr. Evans Eghan and Mr. Isaac Kwain.

This final petition was intensely defended before the Commission of Inquiry whose mandate it was to inquire whether a "substantial demand" existed for the creation of the Bono East Region.

The Commission was hell-bent on doing an independent, objective, and honest assignment for the nation. To the Commission, the other petitions and agitations for regions, such as Ahafo and Oti had been long outstanding with historical grounding, whereas that of Bono East was fairly new and without much history.

The Bono East petitioners argued that the cases being made for a new region by the other five petitions also applied to the Bono East Region. In fact, in some cases those of the Bono East were even much stronger, such as the case of spatial extent and population size. For those reasons, the absence of antecedence of the Bono East petition should, in no way, constitute grounds for disqualification and/or diminish the case for its creation.

Clarifying and defending the Bono East petition further, in his capacity as a citizen of the Bono East Region rather than as a Deputy Minister, Honorable Martin Adjei-Mensah Korsah drew the attention of the Commission to the fact that there was no requirement of time frame or some kind of maturity provisions in the 1992 Constitution for petitions to be considered, accepted, or rejected. Thus, it made the argument of antecedence feeble, and paled into insignificance.

The first meeting of the Coalition of Chiefs for Bono East Region took place at the Encom Hotel in Techiman, where several representatives and sub-chiefs attended. Figure 5 shows the first meeting of the Coalition of Chiefs for the Bono East Region.

*Figure 5:* First meeting of the coalition of chiefs.

Group picture of participants of the first meeting of the Coalition of Chiefs for Bono East Region at Encom Hotel. Among them are Dr. Agyemang Badu (Educationist), Honorable Martin Adjei-Mensah Korsah (Deputy Minister of Regional Reorganization and Development), Nana Bafour Asare Twi Brempong II (Coalition Chairman and Adontenhene of Techiman Traditional Area), Professor Ameyaw Akumfi (Coalition Secretary), Nana Afena Nketia II (aka Mr. Fred Zeini, Coalition Treasurer.)

This first meeting was addressed by Honorable Martin Adjei-Mensah Korsah at the same venue, Encom Hotel.

Figure 6 shows the Deputy Minister of Regional Reorganization and Development, Honorable Adjei-Mensah Korsah addressing the meeting.

*Figure 6:* Honorable Martin Adjei-Mensah Korsah, addressing the first meeting of the Coalition of Chiefs for Bono East Region at the Encom Hotel conference hall.

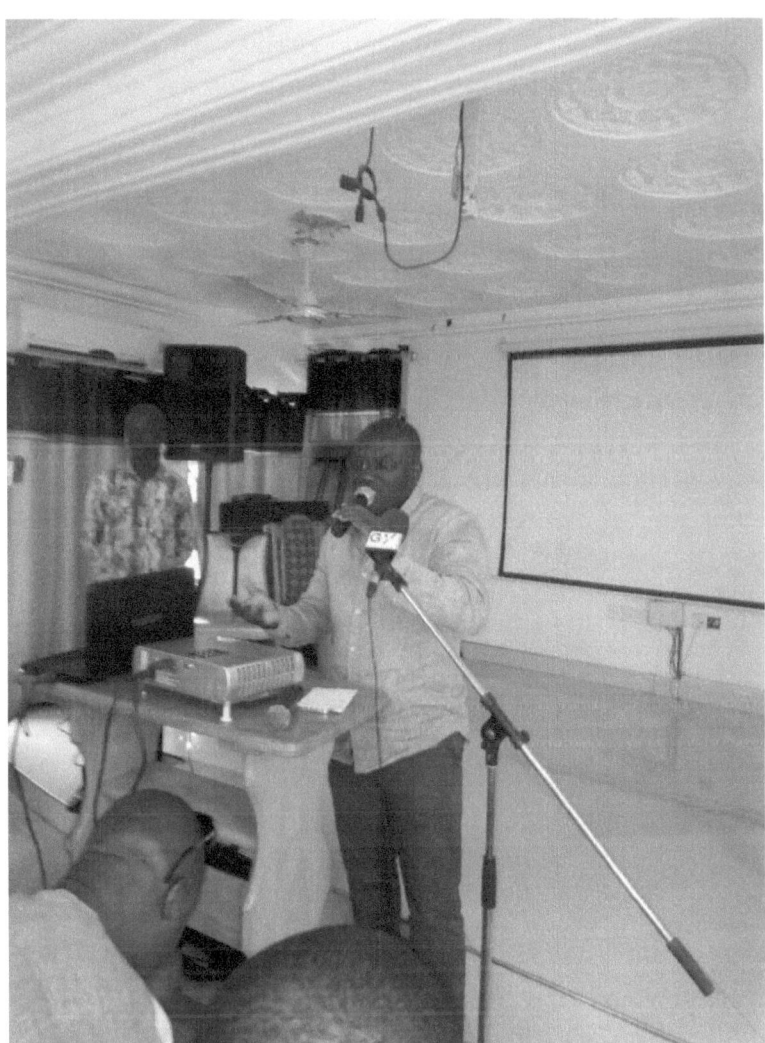

## 2.4 Some Major Coalition Challenges

As expected of any Coalition of such historical magnitude and immense diverse interests, Nana Bafour Asare Twi Brempong II and his Coalition Members immediately came under a barrage of challenges. Among them, some chiefs attempted to form factions on the blind side of the Coalition Leadership to undermine or reverse certain decisions that had already been taken by the Coalition.

At one point, a group decided to petition against the very name "Bono East Region" that had already been adopted for the eastern corridor region. Others suggested "Bono Guan Region," while others suggested "Brong Guan Region," an anglicized version of "Bono." It took enormous diplomatic skills for Nana Twi Brempong II to resolve those issues with the assistance of other Coalition Members and chiefs.

Then Wenchi Traditional Area decided not to be a part of the coalition, with the excuse that it had not been consulted earlier. But according to the Coalition, it wanted to deal first with "substantive" paramount chiefs, under that heat of deadline constraint. Wenchi did not have a "substantive" paramount chief at the time, as the paramount chief had passed into transition and was awaiting the enthronement of his replacement.

The implication was that the already drawn up map of the region that was to be known as Bono East, demographic information, and other pertinent information that the Coalition needed to reflect in the petition had to be revised. This meant Nana Twi Brempong II had to spend a lot of time on revision of the already prepared and time-sensitive petition.

The last thing the Coalition wanted to see was appearing to 'force' a traditional area into the Coalition. If the petition had been submitted with Wenchi on it, all it had to do was to send a protest to the Commission of Inquiry that it was not a part of the Coalition, and the whole foundation of the Bono East project would have come crumbling. It would have raised serious questions regarding the Commission's cardinal terms of reference of inquiring into whether a "substantial demand" existed for a region, right from the outset.

At another point, even right from the very beginning, some traditional authorities had started agitating to get the future regional capital sited within its traditional area as pre-condition for signing the petition to become part of the Coalition. Their arguments centered largely on historical grounds and geographic location within the proposed Bono East Region. All those demanded dexterity in negotiations, as Nana Twi Brempong II argued that if geographic location was the sole criterion used for determining the location of a regional capital, then the national capital, Accra, ought to have been located at Kintampo, the geographic center of Ghana.

Nana Twi Brempong II further argued that several factors are taken into account such as, proximity to other regional capitals, population, economic activity, and the ability of the location to generate funds internally, among others. But for now, what was of utmost importance was to have the needed thresholds crossed in the referendum. So the discussion about regional capital ought to be suspended until after the referendum. Those were very delicate issues that could have derailed the whole project, if Nana Twi Brempong had not handled them carefully.

The Coalition Secretary, Professor Ameyaw Akumfi, had served as a former Minister of Railways, Ports and Harbour and Minister for Education under former President John Agyekum Kufuor. He was once the Member of Parliament for Techiman North. Lately, he had been appointed as the Board Chair Person of the Ghana Infrastructure Investment Fund, by President Akufo-Addo.

He is a biological son of Nana Akumfi Ameyaw III, a former paramount chief of Techiman, who was a leading advocate of the Bono Kyempem Federation that helped with the creation of Brong Ahafo Region.

My encounter with Professor Ameyaw Akumfi occurred while I was on the campaign trail for the Brong Ahafo NPP Regional Chairman position. I had gone to solicit his support, as a prominent and elder member of the NPP, one early morning in August 2017 at his house.

He was quite candid with very useful comments and advice during my brief interaction with him, as we sat at his balcony in his spacious compound. He began by saying that in party politics, it was not unusual for any member in good standing to contest whenever there was a vacancy. He wanted to know about my background and why I believed I could offer a better leadership for the party in the Brong Ahafo Region.

The professor decried the fact that politics in Ghana was fast becoming an exclusive domain of the rich nowadays at the expense of competence. He, however, advised that to level the playing field, I may have to consider reviewing my campaign financing strategies to match the competition.

This, he opined, was because delegates generally tended to act on the mentality that if they do not fleece a candidate while he was eager for their votes, they might not get another opportunity to do so once such candidate gets elected; for he will be gone.

As he was seeing me off, I noticed at his compound a parked rebranded Nissan pickup truck bearing a bold inscription, "Support the Creation of Bono East Region." He appealed to me to vote for the creation of the Bono East Region when the time came.

Following his appeal, I naturally grew curious and inquired about where the regional capital of the proposed region would be located. My curiosity stemmed from the point of view of being an owner of a private basic school, *Oforiwaa Memorial International School* (OMIS), within the Techiman Municipality, which was a potential capital, given its unsurpassed level of infrastructural development, population, access to other regional capitals, and economic activity.

I thought to myself: what a huge competitive advantage it would bring to my school having the potential capital sited in Techiman. Not only would it enhance my opportunity to deliver a state-of-the-art basic school of the highest international standards right to the doorstep of my people, but also an opportunity to leave an enduring legacy that would transmit quality education and training in respect, responsibility and excellence.

I thought it would further offer me the opportunity to develop a school that would mold the character of young people to grow up to be great citizens and critical thinkers. For, I have always suspected that a significant part of Ghana's socio-economic underdevelopment can be traced to the quality of basic education. I also saw in the whole thing the potential of 'immortality' if I could realize those plans for my school and posterity.

The Professor told me that it has not been determined yet, but for now, all the focus was to get the region creation realized in the referendum. His explanation was probably a well thought out form public response agreed upon by the entire Coalition Members that whenever they were confronted with such question, their response should be in unison.

The rational may be driven by their concern at minimizing possible agitations that could result in rancor among the various traditional authorities. And with such a rancor, the unified front for the whole Bono East Region project could come unraveling.

A discussion of the Bono East Region would be woefully incomplete without a discussion of the region out of which it was carved, the Brong Ahafo. So our next focus is on chapter three, which is a discussion of the Brong Ahafo Region.

# CHAPTER THREE

## 3.1 BRONG AHAFO REGION

### 3.2 Historical and Political Background

#### *3.2.1 General Account*

The Brong Ahafo Region came into existence on the 4th of April 1959 by Act 18 of 1959. The Act delineated Brong Ahafo Region to comprise of the northern and the western parts of the then Ashanti Region and included the Prang and Yeji areas that previously were part of the Northern Region.

Before the British conquered the Ashanti Empire in 1900, the Brong and Ahafo states to the north and northwest of Kumasi were within the Ashanti Empire. It can be argued that the Techiman Traditional Authority was a major player of this sphere of influence. The paramount chief of Techiman, Nana Akumfi Ameyaw III, traced his lineage to Nana Akumfi Ameyaw I, whose reign occurred in the period of 1328-63 AD.

The Bono Kingdom had its capital at Bono Manso, during the reign of Nana Akumfi Ameyaw I. The Kingdom thrived as the most powerful kingdom of its time. Nana Akumfi Ameyaw I is on record as having instituted gold dust as a currency and gold weights as a measure. These were later developed and adopted by all the other Akan groups.

Oral tradition has it that nearly all the different groups of the Akans, including the Ashanti people, trace their origins to Bono after migrating from the northern part of Africa, possibly from what may be present day Burkina Faso or even further north of Africa.

King Asaman is recognized as the first to rule the Bono Kingdom, and is generally believed to have led his Akan people from the north to their present day settlement in Bonoland. Later migrations resulted in dispersal of the Asantes, Fantes, Denkyiras and other Akans groups to their current locations. Herein is derived the claim or accolade that the Techiman kingdom is the "first offspring" of the Akan people because all the Akan people and kingdoms originated from the Bono Kingdom.

In 1723, the Bono Empire was defeated by the Ashanti Kingdom, under Asante King Opoku Ware I. The Bono capital, Bono Manso, was completely demolished. Subsequently, the Bono capital was re-located to present day Techiman.

However, in 1935, following a brief reprieve arranged by the British, which brought independence to the Bono States by severing interference in its internal affairs by the Asante chiefs, the Asante Confederacy was restored.

With this new development, it meant a re-subjugation of the people of Bono and Ahafo under the Asante Empire. Although most of the Bono states re-joined the Asante Empire, there was a general feeling of reluctance because some felt their prolonged association never yielded any tangible results in their favor.

Then in 1948 Nana Akumfi Ameyaw III, the paramount chief of Techiman spearheaded secession from the Asante Confederacy. This secession enjoyed the support of some Bono States, notably Dormaa, giving birth to a political movement known as the Bono Kyempem Federation in April 1951 at Dormaa Ahenkro.

Its name was later changed to Bono Kyempem Council. The Council's two major objectives were to demand a separate traditional council and a separate region for the Brong Ahafo states.

Then in March of 1955, Kwame Nkrumah, the de facto Prime Minister informed the National Assembly that the government was considering "the possibility of setting up a Brong Kyempem Council" to fulfill the desire of the Brong people for the establishment of a development committee for their area and that the government would "examine the case for the establishment of two administrative regions for Ashanti." [14]

The functions of the National Assembly were equivalent to the functions of Parliament. Subsequently, a bill was passed in March 1959, known as the Brong Ahafo Bill (an anglicized version of the word "Bono") under a certificate of urgency by Parliament.

The Brong Ahafo Region Act was enacted after receiving the assent of the British Governor General, and Sunyani became the regional capital.[15]

### 3.2.2 Role of Nkrumah in the Region Creation

One account[16] attempted to present the role Kwame Nkrumah played in bringing about Brong Ahafo region. This account largely sought to remove any suggestion that Nkrumah and his Convention Peoples Party (CPP), the most influential political party at the time, planted some kind of the seed of ethnic conflict between Asante people and other Akan groups, especially the Bono people.

According to this account, Nkrumah, as a politician, was only attempting to remedy an issue of historical grievance. It cited the conflict-free coexistence between the Asante and the Bono people since independence, as clear

---

[14]  Ibid., para. 5

[15]  "Brong Ahafo" (2018). Retrieved August 27, 2018 from, http://www.ghana.gov.gh/index.php/about-ghana/regions/brong-ahafo

[16]  Nelson, E. (2013). "Nkrumah's mastestroke with Brong." Retrieved on August 27, 2018 from, https://ekownelson.wordpress.com/2013/08/05/nkrumahs-mastestroke-with-brong/

evidence that weakens the charge of stirring up ethnic conflict among the two groups by Nkrumah and his CPP government in 1955.

This account noted that prior to the early part of the 1900s, the 'sphere of influence' of the Asante Empire, while strong within what was called the 'the true Ashanti states,' also extended to areas lying outside the so-called '50 mile radius' to include places in Bono whose people were subjects of the British Empire. That, the Bono Kingdom were neither under the total control of the British Empire nor the Asante Empire.

This narrative further noted that during the 1800s, some of the chiefs of the Bono areas allied themselves with the British against the Asante Empire. But they could not secure complete independence from the Asante Empire, until after the Yaa Asantewaa War in the early 1900s.

At this time, the Asante Confederacy was suspended, and the Bono people were granted a short-lived separate recognition by the Colonial Government in 1901. This temporary recognition became known as the 'Western Ashanti Province.' It amounted to some form of temporary independence.

However, in 1935, when the Colonial Government restored the Asante Confederacy by returning the exiled King Prempeh I from the Seychelles Island, it marked the end of the Bono States' short-lived independence. The Colonial Government 'forced' the Bono States back into the restored Asante Confederacy.

Some joined willingly and others like Dormaa, Berekum and Nkoranza were reluctant to join. Techiman had to be coerced into rejoining. Even so, some like Atebubu refused to return to the Confederacy.

The general reason why there was widespread reluctance to return to the Asante Confederacy was that it carried the implication of having earlier practices such as, imposition of certain chiefly powers of taxation and levies in areas previously under its jurisdiction restored to Kumasi.

So between the period of 1935 and 1955, this reason turned into a protracted source of resentment and disputes, leading to numerous appeals to the Privy Council of the United Kingdom.

Then in 1948, the paramount chief of Techiman, Nana Akumfi Ameyaw III, decided to boycott Asanteman Council meetings in Kumasi. This action implied a unilateral declaration of 'secession' from the Asante Confederacy. For this act of 'insubordination,' Techiman Traditional Council was stripped of the status of a Native Authority by the British Colonial Government, with its attendant financial and development benefits.

Relying heavily on the support and comradeship of other Bono chiefs, notably the Paramount Chief of Dormaa, Nana Agyemang Badu I, Nana Akumfi Ameyaw III, set in motion his cherished desire for the creation of a Bono-Kyempem Federation in March 1950 to rival the Asante Confederacy.

The main grievances of the Bono States against the Asante Confederacy were that they were discriminated against in the distribution of benefits, with 'true Asante States,' that is, those states lying within present day Ashanti Region receiving more at the expense of the Bono States.

That the youth of Bono States were denied their fair share of scholarships, and that the Bono States carried a disproportionate amount of the prohibition on the planting of new cocoa farms enacted by the Confederacy Council in 1938.[17]

Although, Nkrumah and his CPP had a strong support base in the Bono Area, the Party's response to the Bono-Kyempem Federation was one of lukewarm attitude. Nkrumah did not want a confrontation with the Asante Confederacy or with the Asante King. This politics of avoidance, may have informed Nkrumah's decision not to entertain the pleas of the Bono States.

---

[17] Nelson, E. (2013). "Nkrumah's masterstroke with Brong." Retrieved on August 27, 2018 from, https://ekownelson.wordpress.com/2013/08/05/nkrumahs-mastestroke-with-brong/

With the advent of the establishment of the first All-Black African Government and the excitement that came with it in 1957, the grievances of the Paramount chief of Techiman, Nana Akumfi Ameyaw III, and the Paramount chief of Dormaa, Nana Agyemang Badu I receded from the national spotlight.

Meanwhile, the Paramount chief of Dormaa Nana Agyemang Badu I left on a study leave to the UK, leaving Nana Akumfi Ameyaw III without a committed friend to the cause of the Bono-Kyempem Federation.

Upon his return to the then Gold Coast, Nana Agyemang Badu I was met with new political development and economic agitations.

One was the National Liberation Movement (NLM). The NLM was a political party that had been formed in 1954, by Ashanti members of the CPP. Some of its members included Kofi Abrefa Busia, who later became prime minister in 1972, J. B. Danquah, a major opposition leader against Nkrumah who played a key role in the then Gold Coast's fight for independence, and Baffour Akoto, the senior linguist of the Asante King. These were disaffected members of the CPP.

The NLM was opposed to centralization of political power and advocated for a federal form of governance. It also advocated for the continuing role for chiefs in public administration.[18]

The leadership of the NLM turned into a major critic of Nkrumah and his CPP, especially for its perceived dictatorial inclinations and chose to collaborate with other regionalist groups such as, the Northern People's Party, Muslim Association Party, and the Anlo Youth Organization[19]

It gained the support of voters in the Gold Coast legislative election in 1956. It became the third largest political party in the National Assembly, after the CPP and the Northern People's Party, and won 12 seats.

---

[18] Ibid.

[19] Amankwa, S. E. (2018). "Political party activity in Ghana—1947 to 1957." Retrieved August 27, 2018 from, http://www.ghana.gov.gh/index.php/media-center/features/2888-political-party-activity-in-ghana-1947-to-1957

Although, the support base of the CPP in Ashanti had dwindled significantly, remnants of support remained in the broader Asante Confederacy. However, much of this support was kept suppressed because of the fear of retribution by the Asanteman Council. Any dissention to the cause of the NLM, especially by chiefs, was construed as a rebellion against the Golden Stool of the Asante Kingdom, with possible sanctions of being dethroned.

These developments sent the right signals to the Bono Kyempem Federation to intensify their campaign efforts at independence from the Asante Confederacy.

The other bloc of the NLM was a coalition of rich and powerful cocoa farmers who were demanding higher prices for their cocoa. Significant numbers of those farmers were from the Bono States.

Given the fact that at the heart of all human motivations and actions is self-interest, Nkrumah may have privately cherished some kind of a Bono Union as a counterweight to the hegemony of the Asante Confederacy. In other words, a divide and rule tactics could benefit him, if he eventually emerged as the de jure ruler of Ghana.

Apart from the merits in the case of the paramount chiefs of Techiman and Dormaa, the dynamics have changed, raising the stakes for Nkrumah. He is now confronted with a formidable opposition in the NLM, having its support base as a rich and powerful coalition of cocoa farmers, many of whom were previous disenchanted CPP supporters in solidarity with the Asante King and the Asanteman Council.

He is also faced with the opportunity from the Bono Chiefs to somehow, counter that opposition from the NLM under the name and pretext of "greater Ashanti." He was under pressure from Bono Chiefs who were threatening to withdraw their support for the CPP that won substantial majorities in Bono States like Sunyani, Wenchi and Berekum.

The Asante King and the Asante Confederacy has now taken open side with the opposition NLM and throwing a direct challenge to his CPP government. The foundation of the validity or credibility of Nkrumah's hitherto strategy of conflict avoidance with the Asante King and the Asante Confederacy had been shaken to the core, rendering it useless.

Faced with those choices, in March 1955, Nkrumah announced his intention to consider the following measures:[20]

1. "Possibility of setting up a Brong-Kyempem Traditional Council."
2. "Desire of Brongs for the establishment of a Development Committee for their areas."
3. "Case for the establishment of two Administrative Regions for Ashanti."

As a follow up to those enumerated measures, Parliament, in December 1955, passed the Asante State Council Amendment Ordinance which permitted Chiefs below the status of paramount to appeal constitutionally decisions of the State Council to the Governor against their removal.

This law cut through the very core of the powers of both the Asante King and the State Council to remove uncooperative or rebellious chiefs. The battle lines had been drawn, leading to the subsequent creation of the Brong Ahafo region.

## 3.3 Physical Features

This section discusses the physical features of Brong Ahafo Region, the region out of which the Bono East was carved.

With a land size covering an area of 39,557 square kilometers and being the second largest region in Ghana, Brong Ahafo Region represents 16.6 % of the total land size of Ghana. The region is situated in the forest zone and

---

[20] Nelson, E. (2013). "Nkrumah's masterstroke with Brong." Retrieved on August 27, 2018 from, https://ekownelson.wordpress.com/2013/08/05/nkrumahs-mastestroke-with-brong/

is a major cocoa and timber producing area. The region is also reported to be amply endowed with natural resources.[21]

The northern part of the region lies in the savannah zone and is quite suitable for the production of grain and tuber food crops. With a population of 2,310,983 in the region, it has a growth rate of 2.7%, slightly above the national average of 2.55% for the period between 1960 and 2010. [22]

There are two main vegetation types, the moist semi-deciduous forest, found mostly in the southern and southeastern parts of the region, and the guinea savannah woodland type, which is predominant in the northern and northeastern parts of the region where Bono East Region is located.

These two main vegetation types largely determine economic activity. For example, production of cash crops, such as cocoa and cashew thrive in the moist semi-deciduous forest areas found in the Southern and southeastern parts of the region.

This is not to say that other zones in the region do not support the cultivation of cash crops, but in terms quantity, certain plantations are more predominant due to the vegetation type.

Brong Ahafo ranks among the three largest cocoa producing areas in the country, mainly in the Ahafo area of the region. The region is the citadel for the production of cashew in Ghana, some of which are processed into brandy and cashew wine at Nsawkaw in the Tain District.

Timber also is produced in abundance in the Ahafo area, in places such Mim, Goaso, and Acherensua. Other cash crops grown in the forest area are coffee, rubber and tobacco.

---

[21] 2010 Population and Housing Census: Regional Analytical Report – Brong Ahafo (2013). Retrieved on December 7, 2018 from, http://www.statsghana.gov.gh/docfiles/2010phc/2010_PHC_Regional_Analytical_Reports_Brong_Ahafo_Region%20.pdf

[22] Ibid

The chief food crops that come from Brong Ahafo are yam, maize, cocoyam, cassava, plantain rice, and tomatoes. Yam thrives very much in the guinea savannah zone, in places such as Techiman, Nkoranza, Kintampo, Prang, Yeji, Kwame Danso, and Kageji areas.[23]

---

[23] "Brong Ahafo" (2018). Retrieved August 28, 2018 from, http://www.ghana.gov. gh/index.php/about-ghana/regions/brong-ahafo

# CHAPTER FOUR

## 4.1 DEMOCRATIC DISPENSATION

### 4.2 Constitutional Provisions

Chapter Two of the 1992 constitution of Ghana, states that "the President [of Ghana] may, by constitutional instrument, (a) create a new region, (b) alter the boundaries of a region; or (c) provide for the merger of two or more regions in the country."

The Constitution further provides that the president, "shall acting in accordance with the advice of the Council of State, appoint a commission of inquiry to inquire into the demand and to make recommendations on all the factors involved in the creation, alteration or merger [of a region]."

### 4.3 Concepts of Democracy and Citizenship

Evidence has been adduced to support the fact that governance and socio-economic development are much more effective through meaningful decentralization and devolution of state power. In other words, breaking up governance into smaller units permits effective supervision and inclusiveness than it would be otherwise.[24]

In Africa and developing countries, including Ghana, decentralization is now at the heart of government policies and on-going reforms to bring governance closer to the people, in order to achieve rapid socio-economic development.[25]

Concepts of democracy and citizenship also necessitates that governance be brought closer to the people for the true well-being of all. These concepts have evolved over time and they continue to evolve.

It is the enhancement of participation in governance that Ghana, at independence, had only five regions, which expanded to ten, and today six additional regions have been created, bringing it to 16.

Participation in governance is done principally through the vehicle of public administration. Contemporary public administration concerns itself with a whole new range of evolving issues, as governance is faced with, (a) democratic citizenship or the creation of a governance that involves the voice of the ordinary citizen through awareness, enhanced knowledge, and political activism within their communities using their own mind, (b) service to citizens or providing and upholding the moral and ethical standards that meet the needs of citizens through institutions and bureaucracies, and (c) public interest or the sense of the collective common good within society.[26]

---

[24] Miller, K. I. (2002). "Advantages & disadvantages of local government decentralization." Retrieved on August 28, 2018 from, http://citeseerx.ist.psu.edu/viewdoc/download?doi=10.1.1.134.5990&rep=rep1&type=pdf

[25] Alam, M. & Koranteng, R. (2015). "Decentralisation in Ghana" (eds.). Retrieved August 28, 2018 from, *https://www.researchgate.net/publication/280713246_Decentralisation_in_Ghana*

[26] Chilcoat, G. W., &; Ligon, J. A. (2003-2004, Fall-Winter). "It is democratic citizens we are after:" The possibilities and the expectations for the social studies from the writings of Shirley H. Engle. *International Journal of Social Education, 18,* 76-88.

The avowed purpose of public administration is to develop the best instrument for achieving socio-economic development for citizens of a country. This socio-economic development is also effected through devolution or transfer of any function or responsibility involving both administrative and political decision-making authority, to a sub-national level of government, such as the Bono East Region. Regional administration must be able to exercise autonomy and be free of encumbrances, such as excessive financial dependency on the central government or lack of local administrative and technical capacity.[27]

This enables the new administrative territory or region to initiate its own development projects, as it deems necessary. Being more localized and closer to the people, it is in a much better position to know of opportunities, indigenous resources and comparative advantages on which development can be premised.

Rapid socio-economic development becomes, therefore, locally driven rather than 'externally' driven by the central government, which is usually pre-occupied with many other priorities across the country, and relatively cannot fully focus on local resource potentials for socio-economic development.[28]

But why make governance accessible to the citizens to exercise democratic citizenship? The answer is straight forward.

Human beings do not come into life equipped with 'rights' in our hands. Society rations them by determining the degree of 'rights' that it allocates to citizens and the amount of powers that it allocates to government.

Government is a powerful institution and if citizens do not stay vigilant, the power of government can grow beyond acceptable limits. As one study expressed with admirable succinctness, at the heart of democracy is the

---

[27] Miller, K. I. (2002). "Advantages & disadvantages of local government decentralization." Retrieved on August 28, 2018 from, http://citeseerx.ist.psu.edu/viewdoc/download?doi=10.1.1.134.5990&rep=rep1&type=pdf

[28] Ibid.

assumption that, "our rights and liberties do not come for free, that unless we assume the responsibilities of citizens we will not be able to preserve them."[29]

It is against this background that the rationale for the creation of the Bono East Region emerged.

There were people who advocated that the creation of the Bono East Region was only attempts by the NPP government to score political points and that the exercise will not benefit the country.

They argued that rather, government could resource the existing Municipal and District Assemblies to carry out the function of bringing governance to the people.

Those misgivings appeared to be only intended to hinder the quest by the government to facilitate accelerated national development. It is obvious that Municipal and District Assemblies do have limitations as sub-national levels of governance.

The creation of Bono East Region will serve as a boost for Municipal and District Assemblies to effectively carry out their mandate. For instance, it will certainly impact population dynamics, as industries and businesses relocate or expand their operations into Bono East.

This will swell up the population of the existing municipals and districts within those regions. The resultant effect is that those that become too big get split up into two or even more depending upon the population density.

Thus, the new District Assemblies would join the existing ones to spread socio-economic development across the country through local governance. This will fulfill the core mandate of districts, as drivers of decentralization.

---

[29] Barber, B. R. (1998). *A passion for democracy: American essays*. Princeton, NJ: Princeton University Press, p. 195.

In a democratic state where free speech is guaranteed, it is expected that some will make requests and others will call for their rejection.

Whereas one group of Ghanaians vehemently called for the creation of Bono East Region as instrument for bringing governance closer to the doorsteps of the people, another group advocated strongly against its creation on the grounds of cost.

For example, a member of the NDC, a major opposition political party and private legal practitioner, Abraham Amabila, noted that the country did not have adequate financial resources to finance creation of new regions. He noted further that, even if such funds were available they would be best utilized by directing them to strengthen developmental projects of existing regions.[30]

Another member of the same opposition party and a former Central Regional Chairman of the NDC, Mr. Bernard Allotey Jacobs, held a contrary view. He advocated that having new regions would certainly inure to the socio-economic development of the local residents.[31]

The process of creating Bono East Region imposed certain mandatory obligations on the President. Once such constitutional provision is triggered by the people in the affected area, the President becomes bound to perform certain provisions of the constitution as part of his duties and responsibilities. Failure to perform any such provision may by itself constitute dereliction of presidential responsibilities.

Unfortunately, some observers suggested or insinuated a kind of governmental agenda in the people-triggered demand for new regions. But the fact was that both major political parties, the NPP and the NDC, made the creation of additional regions a part of their campaign manifestos and campaign promises.[32]

---

[30] Dovia, S. (2017). "Abraham Amaliba questions rationale behind creation of new regions." Retrieved August 29, 2018 from, https://www.ghanacrusader.com/abraham-amaliba-questions-rationale-behind-creation-of-new-regions/

[31] Ibid.

[32] Ibid.

Why would they make such promises if the creation of regions were against the provisions of the constitution and had no socio-economic benefits in the lives of some citizens?

The sheer fact of making such bi-partisan presidential campaign promises implied that there were some elements of rapid socio-economic benefits to be derived by the local people if such regions were created.

According to the Electoral Commission, the cost of the referenda to create the six regions was estimated to be 932 million Ghana cedis.[33]

Democracy does not come cheap; it is costly, in terms of financial costs for conducting elections periodically at local, regional, and national levels[34] to maintain governance that assures a voice for the ordinary citizen in politics and thereby guarantee public interest or the collective good within society.

But certainly, it is much more costly to leave governance in the hands of dictatorship. For, dictatorship is not answerable to any cost or priorities of resource allocation to anybody. For this very reason, it does not even consider it in decision making.

Ghana spent the following amounts 23.5 million Ghana cedis, 138 million Ghana cedis, 515 million Ghana cedis, and 826 million Ghana cedis in 2004, 2008, 2012, and, 2016 for presidential and parliamentary elections respectively.[35]

---

[33] Awudi, E. J. (2017). "2018 Budget: Referendum on new regions to cost GH¢932m." Retrieved August 29, 2018 from, https://www.graphic.com.gh/news/politics/referendum-on-new-regions-to-cost-gh-932m.html

[34] Kipo, D. (2018). "There is need for creation of new regions in Ghana and cost must not be a limitation." Retrieved August 29, 2018 from, https://www.myjoyonline.com/opinion/2018/April-17th/there-is-need-for-creation-of-new-regions-in-ghana-and-cost-must-not-be-a-limitation.php

[35] Asiedu G. K. (2016). "This is the cost of elections in Ghana." Retrieved August 30, 2018 from, https://www.pulse.com.gh/news/politics/election-2016-this-is-the-cost-of-elections-in-ghana-id5772116.html

However, it must be borne in mind that the two voting events are not coterminous in terms of delivery of public good. It is like comparing apples to oranges. Whereas a referendum occurs infrequently or a special one-time event that seeks a stamp of ratification for a petition (i.e., expand governance institution to the doorsteps of the ordinary citizens), general elections are regular exercise intended to ensure that the individual citizen office seeker and the democratic processes are sustained on regular basis. Both differ in structure.

Cost is very important. However, an alternative and enduring choice to democracy that better guarantees the public good has yet to be discovered. Marx and Engels communist system survived for only 70 years. Why for only 70 years if it was a much superior system of delivering the public good?

During interaction with the media to update them on the benefits for the creation of new regions in Ghana at Sunyani, Honorable Dan Botwe, the Minister of Regional Reorganization and Development stated that the exercise was not one of achieving any political expediency but that it was an implementation of a constitutional provision that was grounded on need and substantial demand by Ghanaians.[36]

---

[36] Peprah, D. (2018). "Bono East Region to harness economic potentials of the Eastern corridor."
Retrieved August 28, 2018 from, http://www.ghananewsagency.org/features/bono-east-region-to-harness-economic-potentials-of-the-eastern-corridor-128236

# CHAPTER FIVE

## 5.1 THE BONO EAST REGION

### 5.2 Demographics of the Bono East Region

The Municipalities and Districts of Bono East Region are the Techiman Municipality, Techiman North District, Nkoranza Municipality, Nkoranza North District, Kintampo Municipality, Kintampo South District, Atebubu-Amantin Municipality, Sene East District, Sene West District, Pru East District and Pru West District.[37]

The new region broke away with 11 political Districts and Municipalities out of the erstwhile Brong-Ahafo Region's 28 District and Municipal Assemblies.

Bono East Region is densely populated with 904,256 inhabitants. This number of people represented 68 percent of the erstwhile Brong Ahafo Region as a whole, and 10 percent of Ghana's total land size. The density

---

[37] Adu-Gyamerah, E. (2018). "Creation of new regions: Brong Ahafo in perspective." Retrieved August 29, 2018 from, https://www.graphic.com.gh/news/politics/creation-of-new-regions-brong-ahafo-in-perspective.html

per square kilometer is about 38.2 people. The total land area is 25,314 square kilometers.[38]

Table 2 depicts some demographics of Bono East Region:

**Table 2:** *Population Distribution of Bono East Districts and their Capitals*

| Districts | Existing District Capitals | Land Area (Sq. km.) | Population | Population Density (people/ sq. km.) |
|---|---|---|---|---|
| Atebubu-Amantin | Atebubu | 2,264 | 105,938 | 46.8 |
| Kintampo Municipal | Kintampo | 5,105 | 95,480 | 18.7 |
| Kintampo South | Jema | 1,513.34 | 81,100 | 53.6 |
| Nkoranza North | Busunya | 2,322 | 65,895 | 28.4 |
| Nkoranza Municipal | Nkoranza | 1,100 | 100,929 | 91.8 |
| Pru* | Yeji | 2,195 | 129,248 | 58.9 |
| Sene East | Kajeji | 4,893 | 61,076 | 12.5 |
| Sene West | Kwame Danso | 3,262 | 57,734 | 17.7 |
| Techiman Municipal | Techiman | 669.7 | 147,788 | 220.7 |
| Techiman North | Tuobodom | 330.5 | 59,068 | 178.7 |
| **Total** | | **25,314** | **904,256** | **38.2** |

*Pru District now Comprises of Pru East and Pru West Districts

Source: Report of the Commission of Inquiry into the Creation of New Regions (June, 2018, p. 197)

---

[38] Report of the Commission of Inquiry into the Creation of New Regions (June, 2018, p. 197)

## 5.3 Natural Resources of the Bono East Region

Some independent experts, such as political analysts, industrialists, and economists see this new region as likely to fast-track the socio-economic development of Ghana. This is because Bono East Region is considered to be well-endowed with food crops and precious mineral resources, including gold, diamond, petroleum, lime stone, and timber. But most of those precious minerals remain undeveloped.[39]

Geological data from the Minerals Commission points to the fact that large commercial quantities of gold are spread out in areas covering 1,400 square kilometers, such as Mansie, Anyima, Amoma and Nansuano, as depicted on topographical images of the area.

In the Nkoranza Municipality, at Donkro-Nkwanta, a study by Newmont Ghana Gold Limited confirmed large quantities of undeveloped gold deposits that cover a land area of about 2,000 square kilometers. Verifiable information also affirms that diamond deposits exist in commercial quantities.

Seismic study undertaken in 1977 by Shell Texaco proved that there are undeveloped quantities of petroleum deposits at Premuase, a farming community in the Sene East District. According to sources, history shows that Shell Texaco nearly commenced oil drilling at that time.[40]

There is also a special type of clay suitable for the production of clinker for cement and industrial products, such as paint and ceramics in large quantities located around New Longoro, a settler community in the Kintampo Municipality, as well as several other areas in the region that may be tapped for certain industrial products.

The new region is also richly endowed with water resources with the Volta River to the farther east being the main river. Stretching from Kintampo Municipality to the Pru District and through Sene East District and Sene

---

[39] Ibid.
[40] Ibid.

West District, the Volta River serves as the main boundary separating Bono East Region from the Oti and Volta regions, and it covers a distance of about 460 kilometers. This river holds a lot of economic value.

The river is a major source of sea food, especially fish, which can be developed to transform the socio-economic lives of the people who live along the river areas. But, as most of these economic resources are left unexploited, many of its residents still live under very unacceptable socio-economic conditions, with infrastructural deficits, high unemployment, and poverty levels[41]

## 5.4 Economic Activities of the Bono East Region

The Bono East Region is richly endowed with large arable land for farming, having over 70 percent of the inhabitants actively engaged in peasant farming. The region is the leading producer of maize, cowpea, soya beans, yam, cassava, tomatoes, water melon, and cash crops such as cashew and mango.

It also has market centers that offer several varieties of goods and services with the dominant goods being agricultural products. In fact, the largest agricultural food market center in Ghana is located in Techiman, which is within the region. It serves not only Ghana as a whole, but also the West Africa sub-region.

There are other large food market centers in places, such as Nkoranza, Kintampo, Atebubu, Yeji, Kwame Danso, and Kageji, all within the region. They cater to both wholesale and retail trades. Together, they constitute a hub of agricultural food trade in Ghana and the West African sub-region.

These trades are even more facilitated by the fact that the only major international motor traffic road in Ghana to Northern African countries like Burkina Faso and Mali, to name only a few run through the proposed region, thus enhancing trade.

---

[41]  Ibid.

On the light industrial front, the Bono East Region has major factories in Techiman, including Ghana Nuts Company Limited that processes Soya beans, Shea nuts, and cashew nuts into vegetable oil for export. A fully mechanized processing plant for drying, roasting, shelling and grading of raw cashew nuts for export is also located in Techiman. However, it has lately been closed down, but with its infrastructure still standing intact, revamping it into operation may not entail longer process.

There is also a cassava processing factory for industrial starch and gari, a form of staple food, at Atebubu in commercial quantities.

Another industrial activity in the region is the manufacturing of clay products as building and construction materials and for other uses.

In the services industry, the Bono East Region is awash with vibrant financial service sector, including major banks, such as GCB, ADB, NIB, and GT among others. It is also well served by numerous smaller financial institutions, such as rural banks, licensed savings and loans companies, and credit unions.

Among the oldest credit unions is Abosomankotere Co-operative Credit Union, which is very well operated with the state of the art infrastructure. It has excellent managerial competence, with experienced Board of Directors and energetic Chief Executive Officer, Mr. Prosper Aforbu. It caters adequately to the interests of small and medium sized businesses.

There are also international class hospitality industries that provide decent temporary accommodation for business people and tourists. There are very good missionary hospitals like Holy Family Hospital and Valley View Hospital as well as, high standard private hospitals such as, Amoako Healthcare City, Opoku Agyeman Hospital, and Mount Olive Hospital, to mention only a few.

The Bono East Region has good tourist attraction centers, including the sacred groves and caves inhabited by bats at Buoyem near Techiman, the

Fiema and Buabeng monkey sanctuary at Nkoranza, and the Kintampo Water Falls.[42]

The other tourist attraction center, Digya National Park in Sene, is the second largest national park and the oldest in Ghana.[43]

There are also the yearly Apoo and Yam festivals at Techiman that depict rich cultural and traditional expressions among others.

The Volta River to the North and North Eastern part of the region is a major venue for fishing. Fresh tilapia fish are found in large quantities and provides job for the local people and reduces the level of unemployment. This sector has much room for improvement under the new regional administration.

Finally, but not the least, the Bono East Region already has certain infrastructure for a regional administration, regional offices for heads of various governmental departments, ministries and agencies. Hopefully, the new region will expedite the delivery of socio-economic development in the lives of the people. It would also become a major avenue for creating employment for the people.

## 5.5 Human Capital of the Bono East Region

The Bono East Region also boasts of an array of human capital, including highly educated professionals. In spite of this array of human capital, the region has been disadvantaged when it comes to political representation.

Studies pointed to the fact that since the Brong Ahafo Region's creation in 1959, there has been only two substantive Regional Ministers who have come from the Eastern part, which today is the Bono East Region.

---

[42] Ayibani, I. T. (2018). "Chiefs Offers Explanation to the Creation of Bono East Region." Retrieved August 28, 2018 from, https://www.newsghana.com.gh/chiefs-offers-explanation-to-the-creation-of-bono-east-region/

[43] "Digya National Park". (2018). Retrieved on September 20, 2018 from, https://www.revolvy.com/page/Digya-National-Park

Of those two substantive Regional ministers, one of them occupied the position for just 16 months. The Eastern part has had only four Deputy Regional Ministers to date, with the fourth one appointed to office on August 9, 2018.

At the national level, the entire Eastern part of Brong Ahafo has had no substantive appointment at the ministerial level.

Therefore, with the advent of this new region, the chiefs and people are quite elated. They see the enormous opportunity as more than welcome for developing to the fullest degree the economic potentials of this place, and hope that it will attract investments to help alleviate the economic plight of its people and also Ghana generally.[44]

---

[44] Peprah, D. (2018). "Bono East Region to harness economic potentials of the Eastern corridor."
Retrieved August 28, 2018 from, http://www.ghananewsagency.org/features/bono-east-region-to-harness-economic-potentials-of-the-eastern-corridor-128236

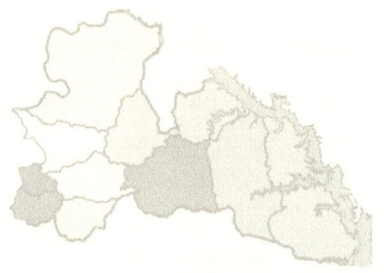

# CHAPTER SIX

## 6.1 DECENTRALIZATION

### 6.2 Insufficient Central Government Commitment to Regional Decentralization

Decentralization may be defined as the shifting of some responsibilities and functions of the Central Government to sub-national levels of government, such as Regional and District administrations in Ghana. The objective is to restructure procedures and practices in order to bring governance to the doorstep of the citizens. Decentralization manifests in several forms, including De-concentration and Devolution.[45]

De-concentration or administrative and bureaucratic decentralization occurs when some of the functions of Central Government are shifted to sub-national levels of government, but ultimate decision making powers remain in the hands of the Central Government.

When the shifting of administrative and bureaucratic powers, that is De-concentration, is accompanied by political decision-making powers,

---

[45] Miller, K. I. (2002). "Advantages & disadvantages of local government decentralization." Retrieved on August 28, 2018 from, http://citeseerx.ist.psu.edu/viewdoc/download?doi=10.1.1.134.5990&rep=rep1&type=pdf

it may be referred to as Devolution. This enables the sub-national level of government to make certain decisions that are free from constraints, such as decisions that enable them to progressively wean themselves of excessive financial reliance on the Central Government or increase the level of their ability to provide their local administrative and technical capacity.[46]

Among the factors that affect creativity, autonomy has been identified as one of the strongest.[47] The more autonomy that can be given to a region, the more the problem-solving and creativity skills get released to maximize productivity.

The real challenge of whether the full potential of the Bono East Region would be realized would largely depend on the degree of autonomy or devolution that the Central Government would be willing to cede to the new Regional Administration.

At independence in 1957, the Ghana Constitution prescribed a unitary system. Even though, there was also a constitutional provisions for Regional Assemblies as a result of public demand for local autonomy, the Nkrumah government was reluctant to grant full local autonomy. This reluctance was manifested through a centralization of political power through the 1960 Constitution and subsequent amendments.[48]

Among the reasons why Ghana's Central Governments have been cautious in ceding complete autonomy may stem from fear of secession, irredentism, and other centrifugal pressures that impede national cohesion. Those fears by Central Government of concentrating political power in the name of national cohesion and minority protection may not be a bad idea in itself; nevertheless, it seriously undermines local independence and initiatives.[49]

---

[46] Ibid.

[47] Solomon, Y. (2018). "Autonomy is important for creativity, but it's not for everyone." Retrieved September 8, 2018 from, http://innovationexcellence.com/blog/2015/07/27/autonomy-is-important-for-creativity-but-its-not-for-everyone/

[48] Asante, R. & Gyimah-Boadi, E. (2004). "Ethnic Structure, Inequality and Governance of the Public Sector in Ghana." Retrieved September 5, 2018 from, http://www.unrisd.org/80256B3C005BCCF9/search/8509496C0F316AB1C1256ED900466964

[49] Ibid.

The Provisional National Defence Council (PNDC) government of John Rawlings appears to have demonstrated a more comprehensive commitment towards decentralization in the 1980s with its policies on the District Assemblies under PNDC Law 207 in 1988. Those policies were later annexed into the 1992 Constitution,[50] but its emphasis was largely on District Assemblies decentralization. Regional Administrations appear not to have received much boost towards decentralization under that law.

Granting full autonomy to Regional Governments does permit them to initiate developmental programs using resources that are peculiar and of competitive advantage to the local communities, of which the indigenes know much about. It frees them of much of the fetters of the Central Government and allows creativity.

The present model of Central, Regional, and District governance are legacies of the Colonial Administration. They were never intended to serve the interest of the Colonial State to achieve socio-economic development. They were rather intended to advance the interests of the Colonialists, which were largely exploitative. At the core of this model was distrust.

They were intended to create dependency on the part of the Colonial State, which was considered to be incapable of self-governance, or making sound decisions regarding its own resource management and allocation.

One study[51] observed that the style of direct and indirect rule by colonial administrations negatively affected postcolonial political development and of consequence the economic development of certain African states, especially those south of the Sahara.

For instance, under the indirect rule, exploitation activities by the colonialists created distrust between the indigenous indirect rulers and

---

[50] Ibid
[51] Lange, M. (2004). "British Colonial Legacies and Political Development." World Development, Vol. 32, Iss. 6: 905-922.

the indigenous ruled class, a situation that negatively affected Sub-Sahara States postcolonial economic and political development.[52]

This mindset persists to this day, laden with the vestiges of distrust, which probably fuels Central Government's suspicion and reluctance to grant full devolution to Regional Administrations. As observed by one study[53], the Central Government has always been wary of granting full local autonomy and self-governance for fear of fissiparous actions that could injure national unity.

Ghana needs a paradigm shift to wean itself from such progress inhibitive mindset. This new paradigm shift must emphasize true devolution and decentralization of political autonomy to the Regional Administrations and make it a cornerstone for erecting a Ghanaian society that will stand out as quite distinct from the past, and truly serve the socio-economic interests of the country.

Ghana is now maturing into civilian governance and restoring the public's trust in governance and bureaucracy that had suffered corruption and the narrow self interests of others.

There is a need for a completely new participatory governance framework of trust, along with adequate scope for local self-management. The country's security has endured stability, and we need to let go of the fetters of fear of secession, irredentism, and other centrifugal forces that impede national cohesion.

Ceding autonomy to Regional Administrations will go a long way to strengthen Agenda 2030 or the Millennium Development Goals. It will unleash the tremendous innovative spirit, leadership talents, and innate problem-solving capacity that reside in Ghanaians. These talents are curtailed by the existing over-centralized governance system.

---

[52] Mizuno, N. & Okazawa, R. (2009). "Colonial experience and postcolonial underdevelopment in Africa." Public Choice, Vol. 141: 405 - 419.

[53] Asante, R. & Gyimah-Boadi, E. (2004). "Ethnic Structure, Inequality and Governance of the Public Sector in Ghana." Retrieved September 5, 2018 from, http://www.unrisd.org/80256B3C005BCCF9/search/8509496C0F316AB1C1256ED900466964

Devolving and decentralizing complete political autonomy to Regional Administrations, with the exception of certain state institutions, such as National Security and Anti-Corruption Agencies will go a long way towards enhancing Ghana's socio-economic development. There cannot be any chaos and confusion, just as there cannot be any chaos and confusion when 275 Members of Parliament represent nearly 30 million people in decision making.

With devolved and decentralized Regional Administrations, such as a Bono East Region, not only would it be able to initialize and make its own resource allocation decisions, but they also do so as better placed to know of opportunities, indigenous resources, and comparative advantages on which development can be premised.

For, without more political autonomy, the Central Government of Ghana, pre-occupied with several priorities for the entire country, would be relatively unable to fully focus its attention on every region's local resource potentials for exploitation, in order to ensure socio-economic development for the entire country.

## 6.3 Psychological Dimension of Economic Stimulation and Industrialization

Stimulation of an economy and industrialization do not always happen under the usual dynamics of spatial economic activity. Economic stimulation and industrialization do have psychological dimension to them. But such psychological dimension cannot be fully deployed, especially by Regional Administrations, if sufficient degree of political autonomy is lacking.

To illustrate this psychological dimension, consider the case of recent psychological moves intended to trigger investor behavior by the Central Government of Ghana:

During a recent visit to China, President Akufo-Addo disclosed to the Chinese President Xi Jinping in Beijing that Ghana was working to issue a 100-year maturity bond with a face value of $50 billion to raise resources needed for infrastructure and industrial development of the country.

This was not anything strange, but it may be rare because it stretches the boundaries for long-term financing.

Here was something the Parliamentary Minority spokesperson on Finance, Honorable Casiel Ato Forson, analyzed in purely economic sense, completely ignoring the psychological dimension of the strategy.

The Minority spokesperson warned that it would have serious consequences on the economy of Ghana, illustrating with the assumption that $50 billion 100-year maturity bond having an annual coupon rate of 7% will cost $3.5 billion in debt servicing annually to the tax payer or $350 billion over the 100-year life span of the bond.[54]

Yet the psychological dimension for socio-economic development of the country is very thinly veiled. A bond is a debt instrument. Multi-billion dollar companies and countries issue them in exchange for financing of certain projects. When governments do that, it is called sovereign bond.

Ghana is not the first country to issue a 100-year bond. In fact Austria, Mexico, and Argentina have done so. Multi-billion dollar companies such as the Walt Disney Company and Coca-Cola are on record to have issued 100-year bonds for $300 million and $150 million respectively.[55]

Most of such bonds do have call provision features that permit the issuer of the bond to repay that debt before the 100 years. Disney issued a 100-year bond in 1993 with a maturity date of 2093, but repayment starts in 2023. This means that Disney has had a whole 30 years to invest the money

---

[54] Awal, M. (2018). "100-year bond will ruin Economy – Ato Forson." Retrieved September 4, 2018 from, https://starrfmonline.com/2018/09/04/100-year-bond-will-ruin-economy-ato-forson/

[55] "Coca-Cola Follows Disney In Selling 100-Year Bonds". (1993). Retrieved on September 21, 2018 from, http://community.seattletimes.nwsource.com/archive/?date=19930723&slug=1712406

it borrowed, and to strengthen its financial position to the point where repayment will never be a problem.

In fact, there is even a 1,000-year bond with companies such as the Canadian Pacific Corporation being on record as having issued such bonds in the past. The UK government is also on record as having issued bonds that pay indefinite coupons, called consols or perpetual bonds.[56]

But why should corporations and countries issue such bonds that outlast the life span of the average person? One reason is to achieve a psychological leverage as an inducement to investors.

For a corporation, who would invest in a 100-year bond if the person did not believe that the corporation will last that long? If there was especially high demand for Coca-Cola's 100-year bond, the implication is that investors have full faith that the company will live to repay that bond some 100 years later. This full faith by some investors is enough to attract other more investors to Coca-Cola to expand its operations and to make more profit to pay off that debt.

For a country, who would invest in a Ghana government 100-year bond for $50 billion if the person did not believe that Ghana is so politically stable and on the path to serious growth for industrialization and socio-economic development to take place?

If there was especially high demand for Ghana's 100-year bond, the implication is that investor confidence is high, which attracts more investor confidence. The net result is more capital inflow to develop the economy, increase growth in GDP, and pay off the debt long before 100 years by invoking its call provision features, which there is likely to be one.

A well-invested loan, backed with financial discipline, would pay itself back to service the debt and lay the needed solid foundation for future economic development and prosperity.

---

[56] Phung, A. (2018). "Why Do Companies Issue 100-Year Bonds?" Retrieved September 4, 2018 from, https://www.investopedia.com/ask/answers/06/100yearbond.asp

The above is only one example of how psychological strategy may be used to trigger investment activities for industrialization, without waiting for solely spatial dynamics of economic activity to drive economic development.

But without a certain degree of autonomy, a Regional Administration cannot deploy similar psychological strategies. That is why the major challenge to the new regions, including Bono East is more autonomy from the Central Government; for, there are countless number of psychological strategies that are limited only by the administrators' imagination and creativity.

This is not to advocate for autonomy for a Regional Administration to conduct, for example, foreign policy initiatives parallel to that of the Central Government. Rather, Bono East Region, for example, is well endowed with abundance of natural resources that can be developed to achieve rapid industrialization, with spillover effects across the whole country. But without substantial degree of autonomy they may not be able to embark upon certain actions that could influence investor behavior for economic development.

# CHAPTER SEVEN

## 7.1 THE DYNAMIC FEATURE OF REGION CREATION IN GHANA

### 7.2 Differences of Self-Interest

Creation of a political administrative region has always been characterized, to some extent, by self-interest which varies among individuals and groups. Those self-interests may assume a more pronounced characteristic under democratic governance, vis-à-vis, autocratic regimes. This is because of the very nature of democracy.

This became quite obvious in the case of Oti Region that ran the whole gamut, from Supreme Court challenges to certain cultural practices that involved matters of the so-called spiritual realms. Differences in opinion and interest constitute the very life blood of democracy. In this particular case, there were petitions for the creation of new regions; whereas, there were also counter calls for their outright rejection.

Region creation has been a dynamic feature of political administration in Ghana since the colonial era. New regions were created as population grew and the need to deliver quality governance through broader decision making arose.

The concept of region creation can, somehow, be likened to the contemporary trend of locating healthcare and education delivery within the communities of consumers. For example, we have the Ghana Heath Service Community-Based Health Planning and Services (CHPS) compound, designed to bring health services closer to the communities. We also have several tertiary institutions having their extension centers or campuses, sometimes located far from the institution's main location.

In the developed countries too, it is not uncommon to find healthcare delivery located further away from the main institution. For example, in the United States, Montefiore Medical Center has facilities located in several communities throughout New York. The practice of extending an institution's operations closer to the communities to serve them better appears to be gaining a currency of international best practice.

## 7.3 The Arguments in Favor and Against the Creation of New Regions

This section takes a look at the pros and cons of the regions creation. It does so by presenting enumerated arguments against region creation and then immediately thereafter, providing enumerated responses in italics, to enhance contrast and readability.

Those contra arguments were espoused by one Professor Kwaku Asare, a lawyer and accountant by profession, who resides in the United States. It was selected because it appeared to be more 'comprehensive' among the arguments that floated around against the creation of the new regions.[57]

By his own admission, Professor Asare stated that he did agree with the petitioners for the creation of new regions on the following grounds:

---

[57] Azar, K. (2018). "Why I am against the creation of new regions." Retrieved September 8, 2018 from, https://ghanaguardian.com/why-i-am-against-the-creation-of-new-regions

1. Their petitions were well intentioned
2. They did raise the alarm about the large-scale poverty that existed in their areas.
3. Their observation that they were unable to access facilities in their respective regional capitals.

Below are the enumerated contra arguments by Professor Asare and this author's enumerated responses to each, immediately after his argument:

**Argument #1:**

"The petitions are [were] based on the false assumption that the mere creation of regions will accelerate development, improve governance and alleviate poverty in the newly created regions. The evidence, however, is to the contrary."

**Response #1:**

*This argument is, somehow, frivolous. Rather, the petitioners made the argument that the creation will bring governance closer to the people in the affected regions. For example, the sheer land mass of some of the Regions made the functions of coordinating and monitoring of District Assemblies by Regional Coordinating Councils difficult. Yet those oversight functions are the very necessary functions that could result in alleviation of poverty in those regions.*

**Argument #2:**

"The petitioners do [did] not show the financing or planning models that justify their optimism. Rather, they implicitly assume [assumed] that there is [was] a pot of unused funds that would become immediately available for the development of the newly created regions."

**Response #2:**

*The Constitution does not require the petitioners to show any "financing or planning models that justify their optimism." How did this argument arrive* at the inference that petitioners *"assume[d] there was a pot of unused funds"* for the development of the new regions? Certainly, the concept of 'many wants but limited resources' is very well wired into every brain by basic practical economics.

In fact, the proposed new region of Bono East is so richly endowed with natural resources and tourist attractions that, by granting a regional status with true and full autonomy, it is capable of initializing developmental programs over time. For example, the Kintampo Water Falls can be developed into an international class tourist center or resort, and with development of an airport for the region, it could become a major source of revenue. The local people are better positioned to know of opportunities, indigenous resources, and comparative advantages on which development can be premised, because they are closer to them.

## Argument #3:

"As a constitutional matter, there is no basis for a referendum because there has not been a showing that there is substantial demand for the creation of new regions."

## Response #3:

There is a basis for referendum. Chapter Two of the 1992 Constitution empowers the President to create, alter, or merge regions, and on the advice of the Council of State appoint a commission of inquiry to determine whether there is the need and a substantial demand for the creation.

The Brobbey Commission of Inquiry, using acceptable empirical methodology, found the existence of a substantial demand for the new regions. This decision was premised on six major considerations, (a) the spatial extent of existing regions; (b) road infrastructure; (c) access to government and public services; (d) economic and employment issues; (e) employment and participation; and (f) ethnic, cultural, and religious issues. The Commission also justified its controversial recommendation that a referendum should be limited to the boundaries of the proposed new regions.

*On the controversial issue of places to vote, the Commission further recommended that the referendum should be held only in the areas within the boundaries of the proposed regions. This recommendation was based on Ghana's past history of plebiscites and referendums particularly in 1949 and 1956, as well as international best practices, citing the cases of Scotland, Southern Sudan, and East Timor.*

**Argument #4:**

"The question of who is entitled to vote in a referendum to create a new region is a complicated question of law. The narrow view that only voters in the affected region can vote is consistent with a federal conception of regions that existed in the 1957 Constitution but is inconsistent with the 1992 Constitution's unitary conception. The broader view that all voters should participate in the referendum, while aligning with the unitary conception, is inconsistent with a literal reading of the 1992 Constitution."

*Response #4:*

*This argument does not state specifically what the complication in the "question of law" is beyond the invocation of "federal" concept of the 1957 Constitution and "unitary" concept of the 1992 Constitution. The issue is about what is stipulated in the reigning 1992 Constitution without confounding it with the spirit and/or the letter of the law drawn from both Constitutions.*

*Any complication as to the intent and/or interpretation of the 1992 Constitution in this regard can best be tested at the Supreme Court. But that is a different issue from the subject of the referendum which has been adequately elucidated under Argument #3. In fact, on November 28, 2018, the Supreme Court rejected a suit challenging the constitutionality of the process initiated by President Akufo-Addo on receipt of petitions for the creation of the six new regions.*

**Argument #5:**

"The threshold for creating regions is appositely high to avoid opportunistic creation of regions that ultimately confers benefits to a few and imposes cost on the many. Thus far, the petitioners have not indicated how the creating of new regions will affect the other regions, especially the ones that are being carved out."

### Response #5:

*This argument does not proffer any cogent reason as to how the creation of regions will be "opportunistic" and will benefit the few at the expense of the many. There is no "burden of proof" on the part of the petitioners, per the 1992 Constitution, to "show cause" as to why their rightful constitutional demands will impact other regions. This argument appears to be borne out of deep seated desire to prevent the region creations at all cost, without really presenting valid reasons. Again, the Supreme Court will be the appropriate forum for how petitioners should show cause per the provisions of the 1992 Constitution.*

### Argument #6:

"Significant resources must be directed to the referendum, which we can ill afford considering our budgetary deficit that has put the payment of some current salaries in arrears."

### Response #6:

*How would dismissing the constitutional rights of petitioners for a new region balance the budget and free resources to pay "current salary arrears"? It is as if balancing the budget to eliminate deficit hinges solely on the referendum. According to the Electoral Commission, the cost of the referendum to create the six regions is estimated to be 932 million Ghana cedis. Democracy does not come cheap; it is costly. But certainly, it is much more costly to leave governance in the hands of dictatorship.*

*A referendum represents an infrequent event, in this case, a democratic stamp of ratification on whether to expand governance institution to the doorsteps of the ordinary citizens or not. Cost is very important but an alternative and enduring choice to democracy that better guarantees the public good has not yet been discovered.*

**Argument #7:**

"A negative outcome on the referendum will not only be embarrassing but will also constitute an avoidable and willful waste of resources."

*Response #7:*

*Why do we have to be thinking in negativity? We have seen millions of state funds being siphoned into private pockets by certain greedy politicians with impunity. No benefit to the state or people whatsoever. Now we don't have to be talking about "willful waste of resources" when efforts are being made to find the best sub-national governance system that assures a voice for the ordinary citizen in politics and thereby guarantee public interest or the collective good within society. Nobody said democracy is cheap. Well, the referendum has come to pass, there was no "negative outcome." In fact, the results proved a "substantial demand."*

**Argument #8:**

"New regions are costly. At a minimum, each must have the full panoply of constitutionally mandated agencies and other government departments — Prison Service, Division of Health Services, Division of Social Welfare, etc. These are substantial costs that would only worsen the budgetary and infrastructural deficits."

*Response #8:*

*New regions also come with reduced unemployment rate, which can increase consumer spending and stimulate the economy. It can also expand the tax base for the country. These costs are part of spreading socio-economic developments. Local artisans and others will be hired to put up those sub-governmental infrastructures, and that will reduce the unemployment rate in the country.*

**Argument #9:**

"Creating new regions worsens our insular proclivities."

*Response #9:*

*This argument is unclear and vague. What is specifically meant by "insular proclivities"? If it involves a worsening of national cohesion, then suffice to state that the country's security has endured stability,[58] and we need to let go of the fetters of fear of secession, irredentism, and other centrifugal forces that impede national cohesion.*

**Argument #10:**

"Districts, not regions, are at the core of devolution. We must rationalize the number of and strengthen the districts while moving away from the regions."

*Response #10:*

*Creating and devolving power to new regions will certainly affect population dynamics, as industries and businesses relocate or expand their operations into them. This will swell up the population of the existing districts within those regions. The resultant effect is that those that become too big would be split up into two or even more depending upon the population density. Thus, the new District Assemblies would join the existing ones to spread socio-economic development across the country through local governance. This will fulfill the core mandate of districts, as drivers of decentralization.*

**Argument #11:**

"Creating new regions dilute the vested interests of the other regions while accreting those of the split-regions."

*Response #11:*

*This argument could have used more specificity. Without that, it calls for a response that can only rely on conjecture at best, as to what constitutes "vested*

---

[58] Azar, K. (2018). "Why I am against the creation of new regions." Retrieved September 8, 2018 from, https://ghanaguardian.com/why-i-am-against-the-creation-of-new-regions

*interests." The "vested interests" that accretes to "the split-regions" ultimately benefit the entire country in socio-economic development.*

*The idea of "vested interest of dilution" of un-split regions only exists probably in theory and in nostalgic sense. Split and un-split regions, each remain as whole regions. It is not as though a split-region is going to rob the other un-split regions of something. For example, how is a Bono East Region or Ahafo Region going to adversely affect Central Region or Ashanti Region of representation at the National House of Chiefs?*

**Argument #12:**

"The dilutive impact will trigger an endless cycle of petitions to create even more regions, which will lead to a slippery slope to the well-known tragedy of commons."

*Response #12:*

*Again this Argument #12 should have been more specific. If the phenomenon that you attempted to describe under Argument #11 cannot occur, then it follows that Argument #12 won't also occur as it is presumptuous or under false premises. That constitutes an argument from fallacy.*

**Argument #13**

"Lastly, I must reiterate that the issues that the petitioners raise are pervasive and true of most places in the country. The solution then lies in a holistic developmental approach, including rethinking our current revenue models, tapping into the wealth of our Diaspora citizens, reordering our consumption and investment profiles, investing in information technology and reliable transportation networks, etc. The solution certainly does not lie in creating more regions, districts, constituencies and other administrative bureaucracies."

*Response #13:*

*Those suggestions appear to be tall orders and sometimes impractical. The remedies that this argument prescribed are of a more complex nature than it seems on the surface. Some regions, such as the Northern, Western, and Brong Ahafo regions were just too large for effective monitoring. Such spatial extent cannot certainly be "true of most places in the country."*

*How do you tap into the wealth of Diaspora citizens when your Constitution does not even recognize their dual citizenship or grant them equal citizenship in order to participate in the political space to help solve problems? Their very source of "wealth" that you mention is acquired from their very dual citizenship status that granted them access to better paid jobs in the Diaspora.*

*How do you reorder what people choose to consume in a market economy? Significant part of the solution lies in creating and devolving power to regional administrations.*

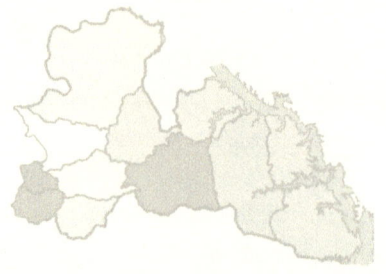

# CHAPTER EIGHT

## 8.1 THE REFERENDUM CAMPAIGN

### 8.2 The Launching

Friday, November 16, 2018 was the day for the launching of the campaign for the Referendum for the proposed Bono East Region, which was scheduled for December 27, 2018 by the Electoral Commission. The event was held in Techiman, at the forecourt of the Bono Kyempem Hall. The main objective was to educate and canvass for 'YES' votes and to maximize voter turnout, which was the major obstacle.

The constitutional provision requiring a threshold of 50% of eligible voters residing in the Bono East part was a major challenge. Once you can get people to turn out to vote, the other threshold of 80% requirement for 'YES' votes was relatively much easier to achieve.

Voter apathy was one thing to be reduced to the barest minimum. To do this, it became necessary for the Coalition of Chiefs for the Creation of Bono East Region to warn voters not to turn it into a partisan affair.

In fact, the spokes person for the coalition, Professor Ameyaw Akumfi, stressed at the gathering that anyone who turned the campaign into a partisan affair would incur the wrath of the chiefs and may be summoned to their various palaces to answer charges of engaging in activities inimical to the socio-economic development interest of the region.

There were several dignitaries in attendance under the auspices of the Chairman of the Coalition of Chiefs for the Creation of the Bono East Region, Nana Twi Brempong II and Adontenhene of the Techiman Traditional Area. Figure 7 shows some of the dignitaries.

*Figure 7:* Coalition chairman, vice-chairman, secretary and other dignitaries seated at the inauguration grounds.

Some of the dignitaries that attended the campaign launching event (From Left to Right): Nana Kwaku Duah, Vice-Chairman of the Coalition, Nana Twi Brempong II, Chairman of the Coalition and Adontenhene of the Techiman Traditional Area, Mr. Kwame Ampofo Twumasi, Former Deputy Minister of Education, Mr. Thomas Adu Appiah, Brong Ahafo NPP Regional Chairman, Professor Ameyaw Akumfi, Coalition Secretary, and Mr. Kwasi Adu Gyan, Coalition Elections Officer.

## 8.3 The Gallery

Several people from different social backgrounds attended the event. The pictures appearing below show the Paramount Chiefs, Queen Mothers, students, and trade organization representatives that attended the event:

Nana Agyapong, Adontenhene of Nkoranza Traditional Area (shaking hands background) arrives with his entourage at the campaign inauguration to represent the Paramount Chief of Nkoranza who had become deceased and a new enthronement yet to be made.

Obrempong Kru Takyi II, Paramount Chief of Abease Traditional Area (center), arrives at the campaign inauguration.

A section of the participants from various ethnic
background at the campaign inauguration.

A section of the participants from tertiary institutions
at the campaign inauguration.

A section of the participants from secondary
institutions at the campaign inauguration.

A cross section of participants at the campaign inauguration

A section of the participants from the Ghana National Association of garages, Techiman Branch, at the campaign inauguration.

The event began with an opening prayer by Pastor Dr. Peter Agyekum Boateng, Rector of Valley View University, Techiman Campus.

Figure 8 shows the Chairman for the Occasion and Paramount Chief of Techiman Traditional Area.

***Figure 8:*** The Chairman for the Occasion and Paramount Chief of the Techiman Traditional Area

The Chairman for the Occasion Nana Akumfi Ameyaw IV arriving at the referendum campaign inauguration grounds.

# CHAPTER NINE

## 9.1 CONCLUSION

### 9.2 The Verdict of Participants at Public Hearings

The participants delivered their verdict on the need and substantial demand for a Bono East Region during the numerous public hearings. It was affirmed by a nine-member Commission of Inquiry that was inaugurated on 17th October, 2017 by President Nana Akufo-Addo, to investigate the need for the creation of new regions in accordance with Chapter Two of the 1992 Constitution of the Republic of Ghana. The Commission, chaired by Retired Supreme Court Judge, Justice Stephen Brobbey, recommended to the President the creation of six new regions on Tuesday June 26, 2018.

The proposed regions included Bono East Region, which was carved out of the Brong Ahafo Region; Ahafo Region, which was carved out of the Brong Ahafo Region; Oti Region, which was carved out of the Volta Region; and Western North Region, which was carved out of the Western Region. The others were North East Region, which was carved out of the Northern Region; and Savanna Region, which was carved out of the Northern Region.[59]

---

[59]  Ibid.

The Chairman of the Commission, at his presentation of his report to the President, commented that if the report was implemented, it will result in the creation of six new regions that will bring socio-economic transformation in the lives of the people.

Figure 9 shows the Chairman of the Commission, Justice Brobbey, presenting his report to President Akufo-Addo.

***Figure 9:*** The chairman of the Commission of Inquiry presenting his report to the President of Ghana.

The Chairman of the Commission of Inquiry Justice Stephen Brobbey (in suit) being congratulated by President Akufo-Addo (right). Other Commissioners included Dr. Grace Bediako, Commissioner (Former Government Statistician), Ms. Gladys Tetteh, Commissioner (Local Government Expert), Prof. Kwasi Kwafo Adarkwa, Commissioner (Former Vice Chancellor, KNUST, Kumasi), Mr. Robert Ajene, Commissioner (Retired Director of Education), Dr. David Essaw, Commissioner (Senior Research Fellow, University of Cape Coast), Prof. George Owusu, Commissioner (Director, Center for Urban Management Studies, University of Ghana), Maulvi Mohammed Bin-Salih, Commissioner, (Ameer, Missionary in-charge, Ahmadiyya Muslim Mission, Ghana), Ms. Josephine Hughes, Commissioner (Legal Practitioner), Mr. Jacob Saah, Secretary (Legal Practitioner), Mr. Martin Adjei-Mensah Korsah (left), Deputy Minister for Regional Reorganization and Development.

The report indicated that majority of public opinion expressed to the Commission regarding the substantial demand and need for a Bono East Region revolved around eight thematic issues. The most dominant issue at the public hearings was access to government and public services, which topped the list with 20.5% of the total number of issues raised by contributors.

The rest were spatial issues, with 18.4%; economic and employment issues, taking up 16%. Others were, road infrastructure, which accounted for 10.6%; access to education, 9.0%; access to health, 7.6%; governance and participation, 13.9%; and cultural, ethnic, and religious issues being the least, with only 4% of all the issues.[60]

Total registered participants and headcount at the public hearings in the Bono East Region were 4,122 and 9,946 respectively. The distribution of registered participants and headcount of participants were Techiman, with 803 and 4,669 respectively; Nkoranza, with 1,018 and 1,890 respectively; Atebubu, with 892 and 1,243 respectively; Yeji, with 645 and 1,044 respectively; Kajeji, with 386 and 564 respectively; and Kintampo having 378 and 536 respectively.[61]

It is interesting to note that Sunyani Municipal, the Brong Ahafo Regional Capital and an area lying outside the Bono East Region, had registered participants and head count of 155 and 163 respectively.[62] Those numbers were the lowest, which may be explained by the fact that the thematic issues of major concern to the petitioners from the Bono East Region did not concern those from Sunyani Municipal. They lived right around the regional capital.

---

[60] Report of the Commission of Inquiry into the Creation of New Regions, 2018, p. 200.
[61] Ibid.
[62] Ibid.

## 9.3 The Early Verdict of Security Services Personnel

On Monday December 24, 2018, the referendum campaign was at its peak. It was only three days away from the general referendum. As is usually the practice with Presidential and Parliamentary Elections, special voting is conducted for security service personnel who supervise over law and order at the polls ahead of the general one.

By close of day, the total valid votes cast by the security personnel from the Techiman Municipality and Techiman North District were 592 votes.

Of this number, 531 voted 'YES' for the creation of the Bono East Region, while 61 voted 'NO.' This represented about 90% of those in favor of the region creation and only about 10% were against.

This scenario was quite re-assuring for 'YES' voters, as this number somehow represented a good sample of how the general voting was likely to go.

## 9.4 The Verdict of Voters on Referendum Day

Polls were opened between the hours of 7:00 AM and 5:00 PM. Unlike the proposed Oti Region that presented some kind of potential security threat, there was not much agitation against the petition in the Bono East part of the county.

There was a general atmosphere of calm at several of the polling stations. The queues were generally short, compared to that of Presidential and Parliamentary Elections.

Figure 10 shows voters calmly casting their votes.

*Figure 10:* Voters cast their votes at a polling station during the referendum.

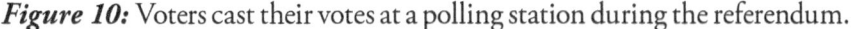

Some voters in a short queue at one of the polling
stations at the Techiman Municipality

When the polls closed at 5:00 PM, people were anxious to hear the outcome
of whether a new region called Bono East Region will become a reality. The

first indication that the YES votes could become a reality was a polling agent's report from Techiman Municipal who posted at his face book page that he was "extremely sure" the YES votes would carry the Referendum.

Then in about 30 minutes later he posted, "sorting and counting finished." Then another posting followed, "YES - 661, NO - 3, Total Register - 472, representing 95.64% of the votes.

It has been nearly six decades since the Brong Ahafo Region was created, so apart from the usual justification of "bringing socio-economic development closer to the people" for a new region; it also presented a rare life time historical event for many people in those affected areas.

By Friday morning, December 28, 2018, people woke up to hear the much anticipated results:

The entire outcome from the 11 districts and municipalities comprising the Bono East Region totaled 450,812, which represented 85.82% of the 525,275 eligible registered voters that turned out to vote.

An overwhelming number of 448,545 voters that represented 99.5% of the total votes cast voted 'YES', while 1,384 voted 'NO' that represented 0.3%. A total of 883 votes were rejected ballots, which represented 0.2%. Those results were declared around 6:00 AM Friday December 28, 2018.[63]

The constitutional threshold required 50% turn-out, of which 80% must vote "YES.' There was 85.82% turn-out, and 99.5% voted 'YES.'

Table 3 presents detailed results by districts and municipalities:

---

[63] "Referendum Results: Bono East Gets 99.5% 'Yes' Votes." Retrieved December 28, 2018 from, https://myarkfmonline.com/2018/12/referendum-results-bono-east-gets-99-5-yes-votes/

**Table 3:** *Referendum Results by Districts and Municipals for Bono East Region*

| Techiman South | Techiman North |
|---|---|
| YES – 100,066<br>NO – 273<br>Rejected – 204<br>Total – 100,543 | YES – 40,653<br>NO – 83<br>Rejected- 67<br>Total – 40,803 |
| **Nkoranza North** | **Nkoranza South** |
| YES – 27,711<br>NO -51<br>Rejected-34<br>Total- 27,796 | YES – 57,166<br>NO – 56<br>Rejected- 60<br>Total – 57,882 |
| **Kintampo North** | **Kintampo South** |
| YES – 45,227<br>NO – 158<br>Rejected- 62<br>Total-45,447 | YES – 32,497<br>NO – 126<br>Rejected- 64<br>Total- 32,687 |
| **Atebubu-Amantin** | **NOT APPLICABLE** |
| YES – 46,668<br>NO – 152<br>Rejected- 72<br>Total- 46,829 | |
| **Pru East** | **Pru West** |
| YES – 33,828<br>NO – 160<br>Rejected- 107<br>Total- 34,095 | YES – 24,133<br>NO – 121<br>Rejected- 88<br>Total- 24,342 |
| **Sene East** | **Sene West** |
| YES -18,318<br>NO – 69<br>Rejected- 59<br>Total – 18,446 | Yes – 22,278<br>No -135<br>Rejected- 66<br>Total- 22,479 |

Source: "Referendum Results: Bono East Gets 99.5% 'Yes' Votes." Retrieved December 28, 2018 from, https://myarkfmonline.com/2018/12/referendum-results-bono-east-gets-99-5-yes-votes/

The remaining five proposals for Ahafo, Oti, Western North, Savannah, and North East regions were all overwhelmingly affirmative for new regions. There was widespread jubilation, not only in the Bono East Region areas, but also in all the areas that took part in the referendum.

What remained now was for President Nana Akufo-Addo to invoke constitutional provisions under Article 5(8) of the 1992 Constitution to give constitutional powers to the results of the Referendum.

A new region, the Bono East Region, has been born.